ADOLESCENTS IN FOSTER FAMILIES

G000146461

Child Care Policy and Practice Series
General Editor: John Triseliotis
Director of Social Work Education
University of Edinburgh

Adolescents in Foster Families

Edited by Jane Aldgate
Anthony Maluccio
Christine Reeves

B. T. Batsford Ltd · *London*
in association with
British Agencies for Adoption and Fostering

For Nancy Hazel

© Jane Aldgate, Anthony Maluccio, Christine Reeves 1989
First published 1989

Photoset by Deltatype Ltd, Ellesmere Port, S. Wirral
and printed in Great Britain by
Dotesios (Printers) Ltd, Bradford on Avon, Wiltshire

Published by B T Batsford Ltd
4 Fitzhardinge Street, London W1H 0AH

A CIP catalogue record for this book is
available from the British Library

ISBN 0 7134 6014 8

Contents

Acknowledgements

First, we would like to thank all those who came to the seminar on 'Adolescents in Foster Families' at the University of Oxford in 1986, and Professor A. H. Halsey for supporting our venture. The ideas and practice provided by the participants at the seminar inspired us to produce this volume. Special thanks go to our authors for their contributions. We also would like to express our gratitude to several individuals who gave advice and other assistance on the production of the book: Hannah Aldgate, Harvey Frankel, Nancy Hazel, Barbara Hudson, Wendy Hurst, Serena Jones, Jane Rowe, Mike Simm, Robert Smith, John Triseliotis and Pat Verity. We are very grateful to the publishers Basil Blackwell Limited for allowing us to quote from Mike Stein and Kate Carey's book *Leaving Care* in Chapter 4, and to the National Foster Care Association, first, for permission to adapt material from their publication *Towards a Discipline in Fostering* in Chapter 3 and second, for allowing us to use the pro forma for agreements in Chapter 7. We are also indebted to Family Rights Group for their assistance on Chapter 7. A very special thanks to all the secretaries who helped produce the book, including Rebecca Dominy, Pamela Harrison, Sharon Ikami and Susan Phipps. We would especially mention Suzanne Jones of the Department of Social and Administrative Studies at the University of Oxford, who endured the various re-draftings of the text with great patience and was instrumental in producing a beautifully presented final version.

The Contributors

Jane Aldgate is a Fellow of St Hilda's College and Lecturer in Applied Social Studies at the University of Oxford.

Anthony Maluccio is Professor of Social Work and Director of the Center for the Study of Child Welfare at the School of Social Work of the University of Connecticut.

Christine Reeves was Director of the National Foster Care Association from 1976 to 1987. She is now Director of Services for the British Red Cross.

Richard P. Barth is Associate Professor and Chairman of the School Social Work Program in the School of Social Welfare at the University of California at Berkeley.

Kate Carey is Research Officer in Social Work for Humberside County Council.

Inger P. Davis is Professor of Social Work at San Diego State University, California.

Edith Fein is Research Consultant and General Partner at the Connecticut Planning Associates, West Hartford, Connecticut.

Tony Hipgrave is Lecturer in Psychology at the School of Social Work, University of Leicester.

Masud Hoghughi is Principal of Aycliffe Children's Centre and a Fellow of Hatfield College, University of Durham.

Marc Jacobs is Director of Independent Living Initiatives, Judge Baker Children's Center, Boston, Massachusetts.

Miriam P. Kluger is Research Associate at Child and Family Services, a Private Social Services agency in Hartford, Connecticut.

Barbara Ann Pine is Associate Professor and Chairperson of the Family and Children's Services Substantive Area at the University of Connecticut School of Social Work.

Martin Shaw is Senior Lecturer in Social Work at the School of Social Work, University of Leicester.

Mike Simm is Senior Social Worker with Oxfordshire Social Services Department.

Mike Stein is Lecturer and Research Fellow in Applied Social Studies in the Department of Adult and Continuing Education at the University of Leeds.

Preface

In April 1986, a seminar was held in the Department of Social and Administrative Studies at the University of Oxford, England, organized by Jane Aldgate, a Lecturer in the Department, and Christine Reeves, at that time Director of the National Foster Care Association. The theme of the seminar was 'Adolescents in Foster Families'. There had been a growing interest in this area of social work practice during the early 1980s, partly inspired by Nancy Hazel and her colleagues, who pioneered a project in Kent to provide time limited foster care placements for young people about to leave care. Following the success of this scheme, others sought to copy the Kent model but often developed their schemes hastily without a sound theoretical base. In 1983, Martin Shaw and Tony Hipgrave from the University of Leicester produced a comprehensive survey of the state of the art (see *Specialist Fostering*, London, Batsford, 1983 – a companion volume in this series). Between 1983 and 1986, little else had been published about how foster care projects for adolescents were progressing.

The purpose of the seminar was to bring together 20 practitioners, researchers and social work teachers to identify and address the current issues and concerns relating to social work practice with adolescents in foster family care. The participants included Tony Maluccio and Miriam Kluger from the School of Social Work, University of Connecticut, who were undertaking a large research study on young people in foster family care. They presented a research-based paper which outlined some of the current concerns in the United States. Several of the British contributors, including Mike Simm and Martin Shaw, presented material on the British perspective.

During the seminar, several themes emerged as important. First, there was a need for a clearly identified theoretical base to guide social workers in their intervention with young people in foster care. Second, because of the dearth of theory, it was clear that, both in the United States and the United Kingdom, there was general concern about young people leaving care (or emancipating from care) at 18, ill-prepared for adult life. The problems to be solved and ideas for their resolution were beginning to emerge from 'consumer' research. Third, it was evident that social workers and foster parents were often dealing with young people with many difficulties and were constantly struggling to find ideas about effective programmes of intervention within the framework of a complex foster care project, unsupported by their peers or senior management. In response to this revelation, after the seminar, the National Foster Care Association in the UK began to explore the feasibility of support groups for all those involved in such projects.

Fourth, what was striking from the seminar was the amount of congruence between the UK and US participants. There was a hard core of common concern about issues such as the training and support of foster parents and the state of young people leaving care ill-prepared for transitions to adult life, controversy about the use of long-term foster family care as a permanency planning option in its own right and, above all, a desire to identify useful theory relating to the practice of fostering, particularly in relation to adolescents.

Although the issues and concerns were similar in both countries, responses to improve theory and practice had developed in slightly different directions. The American writers and practitioners seemed to have much to offer from their emancipation programmes for young people leaving care. Training for foster parents also seemed to be more developed in the United States. By contrast, the British concerns had been more directed towards identifying the theoretical sub-structure for the practice of foster care. In both countries, there was an anxiety about the lack of participation of young people in the care process and about the severing of links between young people and their birth families. With so much common ground between us, it seemed logical to draw as much benefit as possible from each other's knowledge and expertise. Accordingly, Jane Aldgate, Tony Maluccio and Christine Reeves embarked on an editorial collaboration which resulted in the production of this volume.

We can truly say that it has been a most amicable and educative collaboration for the three of us and, to our knowledge, has produced the first publication of this kind in child care social work either in the UK or the US. We were very clear from the outset about the common themes for the book but we were also aware of the inherent differences between our two cultures in style, presentation and use of the English language. To address this latter point, rather than end up with a mid-Atlantic compromise, we have sought to preserve the integrity of style and presentation, paying particular attention to technical terms and spelling. To help readers interpret some of the terms which are discrete to each country, there is a glossary at the end of the book. Additionally, we were very concerned that the book should be useful to social work practitioners; we have therefore included an appendix of names and addresses of organizations, both in the US and the UK, who are referenced in the text. There is also an extensive bibliography. We make no apology for its length since it is a compilation of complementary literature and research, incorporating references from both countries.

Differences there may be but, in the end, these are superficial. What has impressed and reassured us throughout our collaboration has been our undisputed agreement about the fundamental values and theories that underly social work practice in foster care for adolescents in our two countries.

This volume is necessarily selective in its content. It can do no more than begin to address the issues raised at the seminar in Oxford. But if we do not make a start, we are failing the young people and their birth families whose lives are affected by the experience of foster family care.

JA
AM
CR

1   Adolescents in foster families – an overview

Jane Aldgate, Anthony Maluccio and Christine Reeves

As they move toward discharge from care and prepare for adult life, young people in foster families are confronted with the challenges facing adolescents in general plus the demands inherent in their foster care status. In recent years, in both the UK and the US, growing attention has been given to the problem of how social workers may offer the best possible help to adolescents in foster families; the aim of this volume is to identify some of the main issues and suggest ideas to further good social work practice. This chapter sets the scene for more detailed discussion in the chapters that follow: it presents information about the young people and their families, reviews recent developments in policy and trends in programming and practice and highlights key themes and issues for policy and research.

ADOLESCENTS IN CARE AND THEIR FAMILIES – SOME FACTS AND FIGURES

National statistics and various studies in recent years have shown that around half of the young people in foster family care in both the UK and the US are teenagers. In the UK, this was 50 per cent of the 40,773 children boarded out in England and Wales in 1985 (Department of Health and Social Security, 1986) while, in the US, the most recent national survey, from the US Department of Health and Human Services, reported that over 50 per cent of the 276,000 children and young people in foster care (using the term to include residential and foster family settings) in 1984 were teenagers (Select Committee on Children, Youth, and Families, 1986). A more recent study in Connecticut reported that 39 per cent of all children and young people in long-term foster family care were over the age of 16 (see Chapter 5).

The proportion of adolescents in foster family care is increasing in both countries. In the UK (England and Wales only), for example, the percentage of 16-year-olds in foster families rose from 24.2 per cent in 1980 to 27.6 per cent in 1985 (Department of Health and Social Security, 1986), while a survey in the state of Maine, in the US, found that the proportion of teenagers in the total foster care population increased from 46 per cent in 1960 to 56 per cent in 1980 (Hornby and Collins, 1984). In both countries, it is believed that several factors have contributed to these trends, including the fact that the permanency planning movement is successfully preventing the placement of younger children, reuniting children with their birth families, and placing other children in adoption.

Young people in foster care constitute several different groups, with differing needs and characteristics. First, there are those who were placed at an early age and have had a stable career in foster care, typically growing up in the same foster home; second, there are those who were placed at an early age and have been moving from one placement to another, often because they have been described as 'difficult to deal with' and third, there are those who were placed for the first time as teenagers, usually because of their behavioural or relationship problems. The numbers of this last group in particular have been growing in the US, in part because some courts have been attempting to divert young people from the correctional or criminal justice system; indeed, over 25 per cent of foster children in the US enter care as adolescents (Hornby and Collins, 1981; Timberlake and Verdieck, 1987).

According to various studies, nearly all young people in foster care have at least one birth parent living and, in most cases both parents. The families are often characterized by poverty, disorganization and major needs in basic life areas such as health, housing, and education. Moreover, many of the parents have serious difficulties such as substance abuse and mental illness (Davis, 1986; Packman, 1986; Quinton and Rutter, 1984; see also Chapter 5 in this book).

The rising numbers of young people in foster care has heightened societal awareness to the fact that, given their life experiences and foster care status, they face special problems. Borrowing from Rutter (1985), it could be argued that a better title for this book might be 'Maintaining Resilience in the Face of Adversity'. At present, the public care system, both in the UK and the US, has much to account for, if we are to believe the consistently harsh findings from research that young people leave care lonely, without their families, ill-educated, lacking in social skills, and vulnerable to unemployment, various forms of substance abuse and homelessness (Piliavin, Sosin, and Westerfelt, 1987; Stein and Carey, 1986; Susser, Struening, and Conover, 1987).

These findings make a poor testimonial for the effectiveness of social work intervention in the past. But this is the starting point for this book – to identify what are the deficiencies and to suggest ways forward to provide a better deal for young people in the care system or exiting from it. We can identify from the deficiencies that young people need help in *tangible* areas (e.g., job preparation, money management, and finding a place to live) and in *intangible* areas (e.g., dealing with loss and grief, forming one's identity while separated from the birth family and establishing and maintaining connections with significant others). Furthermore, adolescents in foster care need help with preparation for self-sufficiency, an area that has been consistently demonstrated to be a major problem in studies of the views of birth parents, foster parents, social workers and adolescents themselves (see, for example, Chapters 4 and 5).

DEVELOPMENTS IN POLICY, PROGRAMMING AND PRACTICE

Increased recognition of the problems faced by young people in foster family care has led to responses to them by a number of developments in policy and laws, programming and practice.

Policy and laws

First, social policy initiatives, implemented through changes in the law, have tried to provide a clearer foundation for social work responses to young people in care. In the US, the most pertinent federal laws are Public Law 96–272, the Adoption Assistance and Child Welfare Act of 1980 and Public Law 99–272, the Independent Living Initiative of 1986. The former law, reviewed in detail in Maluccio, Fein, and Olmstead (1986), establishes the legal and policy framework for children and young people coming to the attention of the public child welfare system. In relation to adolescents, one of the most significant provisions of this law is its emphasis on the responsibilities of public agences to provide a permanent family for every young person.

On the other hand, the Independent Living Initiative of 1986 focuses on preparation of young people in care for 'emancipation' or 'independent living', that is, the status of adulthood and self-sufficiency. The law provides a sum of $45,000,000 per annum, available to the states to support independent living programmes. It requires that the effectiveness of these programmes be documented, in order for funding to be continued or expanded beyond 1988.

The philosophy and policy of child care legislation in the UK has evolved over four decades. There is generally a distinction made between compulsory and voluntary intervention, characterized by use of the Children and Young Persons Act 1969 and The Child Care Act 1980 respectively, although there is some overlap between the two. Permanency planning, as we now know it, was introduced formally into British legislation in 1975, when a new Children Act (now incorporated into the Child Care Act 1980 and other pieces of legislation) introduced the idea of a 'welfare principle' for children in care – that social workers, in making decisions about children, should take into consideration their long-term needs throughout their childhood and should also consult children about such decisions, according to their age and understanding.

While there is no doubt that this legislation had a significant impact on preventing the drift of young children into long-term care, it was criticized on the grounds that it intended to divert workers from preventing children entering care in the first place (although legislation for this purpose has been in existence since 1963), and that it did not address the problems of maintaining links between children and parents in care. Accordingly, in 1983, the Department of Health and Social Security issued guidelines on maintaining access to children by parents and gave parents more rights to appeal through the courts against the termination of their access. Currently, in the UK, the whole child care law is under review so that it is difficult to give a coherent picture at this time. Nevertheless, the proposed changes may well have a significant impact on improving the care situation for adolescents and their families, first, by formally stressing the value of partnership between birth families and carers in voluntary care cases, and second, by introducing new regulations on the selection and supervision of foster homes, to include more emphasis on education, cultural and racial origins and on making agreements between all parties.

Knowledge about adolescents

Concern about the large population of adolescents who become the clients of social workers has not only led to changes in the law but has inspired initiatives to improve the knowledge base of social workers and their methods of social work intervention, both with adolescents in general, and consequently, with adolescents in care. In the UK, for example, over the past two years one group of social workers and managers in the personal social services has been trying to identify the skills and knowledge they need in order to work with young people. This 'adolescence project' has been a national training initiative funded by the Department of Health and Social Security and sponsored by the National Council of Voluntary Child Care Organizations and the Central Council for Education and Training in Social Work. The project has focused on ten topics which represent current concerns about adolescents with whom social workers deal:

– understanding adolescence as a life stage;
– developing counselling skills;
– handling disruptive behaviour;
– working with young women;
– developing anti-racist practice;
– evaluating personal interactive skills;
– needs of sexually abused adolescents;
– skills in direct work with young people;
– working with adolescents and their families;
– need for appropriate support and supervision.
(Gildersleeve, 1988)

Emancipation from care

The interest in adolescents in general, alongside practice experiences and research findings on the difficulties faced by young people emancipating from care, has already led to certain changes in policy. The most prominent of these involves growth of – and support for – emancipation programmes to prepare young people for leaving care, as reflected in the Independent Living Initiative in the US. Similarly, in the UK, resources for adolescents in care have often been directed at the development of specialist foster care to prepare young people for emancipation from care. The proliferation of UK foster care schemes developed for this purpose was influenced by a project set up in Kent in the early 1980s. The success of the Kent scheme, which was designed to provide foster placements as a bridge to independence (Hazel, 1981), influenced others but, unfortunately, some were developed quickly without serious consideration being given to their purpose and content and, consequently, have not been as successful. Those which were developed

17

thoughtfully in response to local need have been more enduring and valuable.

The development of specialist foster care practice in general

Preparation of young people for emancipation from care represents only one of the many developments in specialist foster care. Indeed, the diversity which these specialist 'treatment' schemes now offer is to be applauded, provided that they are clear in defining their purpose and boundaries. Some of these projects have, for example, concentrated on reparation work – helping children and young people come to terms with past experiences – or on preparing younger children for permanency through adoption, or on assessment of youngsters. The differing use of specialist foster family care has been reviewed by Shaw and Hipgrave (1983) in a companion volume in this series. We do not wish to replicate that work since, to our knowledge, their definitions and descriptions still hold. Current UK research on Child Care Outcomes being undertaken by Jane Rowe (details available from British Agencies for Adoption and Fostering) suggests that, since the time of Shaw and Hipgrave's review, the rapid expansion has slowed down and consolidated.

Specialist and mainstream foster care

In both the UK and the US, it is by now widely recognized, however, that, while treatment foster schemes can be successful, they serve only a minority of the foster adolescent population. Many adolescents in care are in mainstream placements or in residential child care facilities. Yet these young people often have the same problems and developmental needs as adolescents in specialist placements. Furthermore, sometimes social workers have suggested that the decision about 'where to place' relates not so much to the severity of problems but more to the availability of specialist placements when they are needed. This has been a cause of some concern to both practitioners and researchers.

Rights of young people and birth families

Another prominent issue, particularly in the UK since 1975, has been a concern for the greater involvement of young people themselves in the decision-making which affects their lives. This development has been promoted through pressure groups such as the National Association of Young People in Care, Black and in Care and The Voice of the Child in

Care, which have brought to the attention of both professionals and public the views of young people who have exited from the care system. In line with this greater involvement has been a move towards more open accountability in social work agencies, reflected in young people gaining access to their social work files (see MacVeigh, 1982). The UK does not have the same legislation on open access to files that exists currently in the US, but there are strong debates in existence on freedom of access to information held by public authorities.

Not only have young people themselves been asserting their views but organizations, like the Family Rights Group, have taken up the issue of the rights of clients on behalf of parents of children in care. This advocacy has focused, first, on promoting parents' rights, particularly in relation to access to their children in care, and second, on urging authorities to look again at the value of ensuring that young people who come into care maintain links with their birth families.

KEY THEMES AND ISSUES

This book then is presented at a time of change in many areas. It attempts to reflect those trends and to promote ideas about theory related to fostering and social work practice which may encourage the development of better services for young people and their families. It also attempts to discuss how these changes will impact on the providers: foster parents, social workers and other professional staff.

The right to live in a family

The ethos of the book is rooted in the belief that adolescents in care not only require the same opportunities for making successful transitions into adulthood as their non-care counterparts but that they also have a right to live in a family. This right was recently made explicit in the Foster Care Charter issued in March 1988 by the National Foster Care Association in the UK.

The National Foster Care Association believes that all children and young people needing substitute care, whatever their physical or mental abilities, should have the opportunity to live in a family. This does not preclude the use of residential care for treatment purposes for specified periods. Children and young people who are fostered deserve the highest standards of care and it is the responsibility of all those involved to provide a high quality service. To achieve this, the following principles are embodied in the Foster Care Charter:

1 Foster care must be a partnership among the carers, social workers and the placing agency, with all working together in the best interests of children and young people. Wherever possible this partnership should extend to children or young people in care and their parents or interested relatives.

2 The cultural, racial and religious identities of children and young people, their parents and foster carers must be respected in the development of the foster care service and in the making and support of individual placements.

3 Children and young people have the right to continuity in their lives so that their identity can be maintained and developed, their physical and mental well-being promoted and their full potential achieved.

4 The true cost of caring for a foster child or young person must be met and foster carers given the opportunity to receive payment for their time, energy and skills.

5 Foster carers and social workers have a right to preparation for their job and a responsibility to use training opportunities to develop their knowledge and skills.

6 Carers, social workers, children and young people in care and their parents must be able to call upon the placing agency for support.

7 The responsibilities of the placing agency to the foster carers, the purposes and goals of each placement, and the responsibilities of all parties must be stated in writing.

8 Formal decisions relating to individual children and young people in foster care should be taken in full consultation with them, their parents, and the foster carers.

9 Foster carers, children and young people and their parents should be able to challenge decisions and plans proposed by the fostering agency and be made aware of the procedures whereby they can exercise their right of challenge.

10 Young people leaving care must be offered agency services which recognize that all young people continue to need support into adulthood.

(National Foster Care Association 1988)

The Charter is very helpful in clarifying the difference between fostering and other forms of parenting, such as guardianship or adoption; it also leads to a reinstatement of *planned* long-term fostering (defined as a placement of more than two years) as a viable option for certain young people in care. During the late seventies and early eighties, this type of placement fell into disrepute on the grounds that it had led to the drift of children into impermanent, unspecified long-term care. It was argued that the aim of social work intervention was to secure legal permanence for all children and young people in care, whether this was with their own birth families or through adoption or custodianship. But in the last few years there has been a questioning of this view, in light of new research findings which suggest adoption may not be appropriate for all older children and youngsters in care (see Chapter 5). This has resulted in a resurgence of a new version of long-term fostering, with more clearly defined boundaries, which offers an inclusive model of family care for young people, where foster parents are working to enhance rather than sever links with birth families.

Permanency planning – a redefinition

The new face of fostering has brought with it a growing emphasis on the professional task of foster parents for adolescents: to help young people make successful transitions into adulthood. It has also led us to offer a redefinition of permanency planning, couched in broader terms. Permanency planning for children in general has been defined as:

> The systematic process of carrying out, within a brief time-limited period, a set of goal-directed activities designed to help children live in families that offer continuity of relationships with nurturing parents or caretakers and the opportunity to establish life-time relationships. (Maluccio, Fein and Olmstead, 1986, p. 5)

As implied in this definition, permanency planning draws from a philosophy underscoring the value of rearing children in a family setting, a theoretical perspective stressing that stability and continuity of relationships promote a youngster's growth and functioning, and finally, on programmes and methods focused on contracting, decision-making and goal planning.

In relation to adolescents, the definition of permanency planning needs to be expanded and refined even further, so that it becomes more dynamic and, on the one hand, accounts for the main developmental needs of adolescents and, on the other, makes maximum use of resources which may be offered by social workers to help adolescents achieve successful emancipation from care. Such a redefinition embraces three main elements:

1 It is necessary for young people to have an understanding of their genealogical roots and a sense of physical and psychological connection with their kinship system, that is to say their birth families.

2 For young people to maximize their talents they need to have a clear sense of self-worth, self-confidence and be equipped adequately for adult life, partly through acquiring tangible life skills, including education, and partly through cultivating an ability to make sustained relationships with adults and peers.

3 Young people in care moving towards emancipation at 18 need to have a place of stability, preferably located in a family, which they have a right to use and from which they may move at their own pace into adult life.

Generally, young people who stay within their own kinship system find that the primary provider of these three elements is their birth family. Allowing for considerable diversity in family types and inter-actions, many birth families offer a stable location from which their young people may come and go, more often the latter, to test themselves out and build up their self-confidence knowing they have the back-up of adults whom they can trust. Even if relationships between parents and youngsters are subject to the normal turbulence of adolescence, there is always a place to come back to, someone to provide advice when needed, somewhere to leave belongings, someone to borrow money from in an emergency and an adult a youngster can count on if he or she is in trouble. Proximity to adults in this stable location may not be important at all times, as Millham and his colleagues (1986) have pointed out from their studies of children in boarding schools. What is important is that young people know there are adults who will intervene on their behalf when necessary.

Adolescents in foster family care are often in danger of losing this sense of permanence. Child welfare agencies, with their parenting roles shared between several individuals, cannot replicate birth families for children and young people in their care. The purpose of public care, therefore, is to provide for youngsters an *alternative* system of relationships with adults which supplements, to a greater or lesser degree and over a specified period of time, what the birth family can offer. However this is done it is essential that there is at least one relationship between an adult and the young person, which is characterized by its partiality, making that adolescent feel special and important.

Even though, at least in the UK, there are still a number of quasi-adoptive, indeterminate length, long-term foster care placements in existence which pre-date the development of permanency planning as we now define it, the emphasis should not be on trying to create for the majority of young people in care a second family which will replace the birth family. First, this is inappropriate, for foster families are increasingly striving to be seen as professionals, working in partnership with birth families and social workers. Second, for an adolescent who enters care with a multiplicity of problems, it may not always be appropriate or possible to offer a solution to those problems within the confines of one foster family. Help may be needed from a variety of sources.

Take, for example, at one end of the scale, the increasingly large number of adolescents who are coming into care for the first time. Their entry is often characterized by behaviour problems, confusion about relationships with their birth families, delinquency and sometimes, substance abuse. Birth families may feel a sense of relief that the authorities have taken their 'unruly' adolescents off their hands but, nevertheless, will usually wish to maintain an interest in their welfare. If there are several problems to resolve, it may be necessary to deal with these one at a time. Each will require a different treatment model of intervention, often within a different location, all working to a common aim: reunification of the young person with his or her birth family or achieving successful self-sufficiency. In these cases, it may be more appropriate to offer multiple family placements, where several foster families offer specialist help, possibly interspersed with short periods of residential treatment. Such a scheme is currently being piloted in the UK in Kent, under the title of 'A Multiple Bridge to Family Placement'. Additionally, where the permanent family is the birth family, workers will need to engage in an active programme of counselling or other intervention with birth family members to parallel the treatment which is ongoing for their youngsters.

At the other end, there are the adolescents who came into care as young children, and have lived with one foster family for many years, drifting into long-term care, more by default than design. Their contact with birth families has been allowed to lapse and they are strongly attached to their foster families emotionally, but neither the young person nor the foster family wishes to change their legal status in relation to each other. Here, the permanent family will obviously be the foster family; it will be in the interests of the adolescent to remain with them as long as possible, even if this extends after official care ends.

In between, there will be adolescents who have been in care for several months or even years and have had a series of placements. For these youngsters, the provision of a 'permanent' family remains most problematic. Consequently, they require special attention to provide them with a family that is prepared to offer them a stable base. They may not always live with the family, but will know that this family's location is their 'home' from which they can gradually move to self-sufficiency in their own time, as would be the situation for many of their non-care counterparts. For these youngsters, the permanent family would preferably be their birth family but, if relationship difficulties are too entrenched or have been severed by default, alternatively, it might be a foster family.

What we are arguing, therefore, is that, within the care system, an adolescent needs at least one caring adult, who will provide permanence in the terms we have defined and will take on the role of a 'stability family'. But there should be no expectation that this family will necessarily provide all the nurturing, skills training or remedial treatment that some adolescents in care may need. Permanency planning will be dynamic. Perhaps 'permanency' is a misnomer; for this group of young people we might more profitably talk about 'stability' planning, geared to their changing needs. These ideas are explored further in Chapters 4 and 5.

The use of planned long-term foster care for permanency planning

One area, which has been re-evaluated and developed to support the idea of stability planning, is the use of long-term foster family care as a preferred permanency or stability option for young people in care. We wish to endorse the case for the reinstatement of planned long-term foster family care for older children, redefined into an inclusive partnership, as in the National Foster Care Charter outlined above. One example of the potential for this kind of fostering is put forward in Chapter 5, drawing on material from a new study from Connecticut.

Ecological perspective and competence orientation

The broader definition of permanency planning outlined in the preceding section builds on an ecological perspective and a competence orientation to social work theory and practice. The ecological perspective uses ecology as a metaphor. Its essence is that human beings are involved in continuous, dynamic transactions with their environment. Such a perspective provides us with a broad conceptual lens for understanding and working with adolescents and their families.

The competence orientation complements the ecological perspective. It stresses that human beings have an innate drive to achieve competence in their dealing with environmental challenges. It supports practice methods and strategies that promote the effective functioning of children, parents and families. (For detailed discussion of this approach see Germain and Gitterman, 1980; Maluccio, 1981; Garbarino, 1982; Hartman and Laird, 1983; Whittaker and Garbarino, 1983.)

Preparation for life after foster care

Whatever theoretical perspectives we may adopt, it is clear that the main efforts of social workers and foster families should be directed at preparing young people for life after foster care. This is a major theme of this book. In Chapters 4 and 5 the authors reaffirm the evidence about the deficiencies of care, as seen from the perspectives of the main consumers of the care system, and offer ideas for improvement from young people and their families. In Chapter 8, there are reports on the progress that has been made in tangible areas such as accommodation schemes to prepare young people for transition to adulthood.

Although ideas for improving the care system for those within it are important, there is a more fundamental problem, which is more entrenched – a misplaced philosophy which believes that young people should be able to leave care at eighteen and flourish independently. Often these are the very young people who are least prepared for adult life at this point. It seems wrong that they should be forced to exist on their own when many of their non-care counterparts expect to be able to stay within a 'stability family' for as long as they wish until they are psychologically and chronologically ready for independence. Indeed, as shown in Chapter 4, when they do not have access to a birth or alternative family, many young people attempt to replicate this family life for themselves by moving into other people's families – either through being in lodgings or 'adopting' the families of their friends. It therefore seems logical to suggest that we should reframe our expectations for young people emancipating from care. Preparation for independent living should be redefined as preparation for *interdependent* living. (See also Maluccio, Krieger and Pine, in press; Stein and Carey, 1986.)

Looking at emancipation from care in this way reinforces the concept of a 'stability family' who will provide a flexible home base for young people who have reached the age of 18. As already suggested, this stable base could be with the birth family; alternatively, for many young people who have only tenuous links with their birth families, it is a resource that can be offered successfully by foster families. Many foster families do this already, informally, but we argue in several of the chapters that there is a strong case for agencies actively promoting the creation of 'sustained relationships' (Stein and Carey, 1986) for young people emancipating from care, by giving foster families extended emotional and financial support to give youngsters the optimal chance of making a smooth transition into adulthood.

Maintaining links with birth families

Although foster families may take on the role of primary stability families for some young people in care, every effort should be made to preserve for the majority of young people links with their families of origin. Here we are defining 'links' in a very general sense, as opposed to 'contact', which is defined by physical meetings between parents and young people. The argument for maintaining links is already strong. Links counteract feelings of genealogical bewilderment, enhance identity and provide a psychological base when young people leave care. Accounts of isolation and dislocation by young people who have left care, like those described in Chapter 4, are enough in themselves to provide cogent arguments for offering every opportunity for young people to maintain links with their birth families, including their siblings and extended family members and their communities.

New research evidence suggests that there can be even more compelling reasons for pursuing this policy, since birth families may often provide the only chance of permanence for young people when they leave care (Jones, 1983; Milham, Bullock, Hosie and Haak, 1986; Thoburn, Murdoch and O'Brien, 1986).

The case for maintaining links between birth families and young people is developed in several chapters in this book. This approach does not deny the difficulties inherent in maintaining physical contact between young people in care and their families and it actively asserts that young people should have freedom of choice in the extent to which they maintain actual contact. For some young people who have alienated not only their family but their teachers, the police and other members of their local community, a temporary 'fresh start' may be positively therapeutic. Young people have a right to air their views in this matter. They also have a right to reject temporarily contact with their families face-to-face. Some may also wish to sever all links permanently but drastic action should be avoided wherever possible. Furthermore, even a temporary termination of links should in no way reflect any explicit or implicit collusion from foster parents or social workers. We believe very firmly that, wherever possible, the door should be kept open for young people to return to their families, although we recognize that, in some cases, where young people have been in care virtually all their lives or where they have been abused, this may be unrealistic. But, there is no substantial research evidence to demonstrate that children cannot live successfully in one family while maintaining links or direct contact with another, whether this be in adoption, foster care, or in families where parents have divorced (see Aldgate and Simmonds, 1988).

There are, of course, many reasons why young people come into care in the first place but we know that, often, family breakdown is caused by unsatisfactory interaction between parents and children as well as by environmental stress. Nevertheless, we feel that every effort should be made by social workers to help parents in their own right so that their potential for change may be exploited (see Maluccio and Sinanoglu, 1981; Sinanoglu and Maluccio, 1981; Family Rights Group, 1986). In time, some parents find themselves naturally at a different stage of their life cycle and more able to manage and relate appropriately to their older offspring. By the time young people have reached the age of 18, they too may have matured and be more responsive to change in their parents. But, in many cases, as suggested in Chapters 4, 5 and 6, parents will need help to make these changes. This can come both from social workers, through their direct intervention, and from foster families who may nurture them, teach them new skills and include them in a partnership whose ultimate aim is to achieve reunification.

In this book, particularly in Chapters 4 and 6, we attempt to take forward ideas about how birth families may be involved with their youngsters in care. Written agreements are a useful tool to this end, as considered in Chapter 7, but their success will depend on the way they are constructed and on the motivation and activity of all those concerned, including the social worker. Indeed, as shown in the Kent special family placement scheme (Hazel, 1981) and in recent research on effecting permanence for older children (Thoburn, Murdoch and O'Brien, 1986), social work activity may be the most influential variable for the achievement of a successful outcome.

The right of young people to participate in decision-making

What we have suggested is that, within the ecological perspective, there is room for considerable variation of relationships between parents, foster parents and young people. These will be determined by young people's prior experiences, factors which led to their removal to foster family care, and their own wishes. One of the significant issues that arises from consumer studies is the right of young people to take a substantial part in the making of decisions which affect their lives. By definition, these youngsters are 'young people', not children, and therefore should be afforded the kind of responsibility and opportunity for negotiations that are often an accepted part of life for their non-care counterparts. Young people's views on this matter are explored in Chapter 4.

Similarities between adolescents in care and adolescents in general

We need to set the problems of young people in foster care in the context of what happens to adolescents in the community at large. The fact that adolescents in foster care have similar problems and strengths to adolescents in general is, therefore, another main theme, which is taken up in Chapter 2. All adolescents face common problems and challenges in such areas as physical and sexual abuse, pregnancy, unemployment, educational attainment, substance abuse, etc. In addition, young people in care share many of the developmental problems of adolescents in general but have the added dimension of being away from their own families, sometimes compulsorily, with all the accompanying difficulties that this may bring.

A disciplined approach to intervention

Social workers have much to contribute to the well-being of young people in care. Therefore, another major theme of the book is the social work role in relation to foster family placements for adolescents. First, social workers have a duty to offer the best possible services to young people and their families, by developing a disciplined approach to intervention, which draws its knowledge base from the social sciences primarily and which attempts to integrate theory and practice. This concept is elaborated in Chapters 2 and 3. Only with such a discipline can we identify what are the differing qualities and problems of each adolescent in foster family care.

Second, a major part of the social work role is to engage in direct intervention with young people and their birth families. What is clear from existing research is that we are only just beginning to build up expertise in this area. The way forward seems to be through good social work practice, and more evaluation of successful practice experiments is needed. Ideas for the development of good practice are discussed in

Chapters 6 and 7, paying special attention to the use of agreements as a fundamental part of the enabling process.

Increasingly, concern has been expressed about the move towards the use of compulsory measures of care, particularly in the UK, which inevitably brings into question the enabling aspect of the social work role. In our opinion, the positive use of authority is not incompatible with the role of enabler, provided it is overtly acknowledged. Accounts of successful work with ambivalent parents are proof of the value of this approach (see Maluccio and Sinanoglu, 1981).

Finally, social workers have to address issues related to the recruitment, support and training of foster families. Some new ideas about selection are explored in Chapter 9, while in Chapter 10, there is guidance on the key tasks social workers should undertake in their role as enablers for foster families.

All adolescent foster placements should be special

In spite of the fact that we seem to be at the beginning of developing expertise in direct work with foster adolescents (see Chapter 6) we do know more about specialist foster family care for adolescents from the various evaluations of projects which have been published (see Shaw and Hipgrave, 1983). This knowledge has led to a recognition that, because of the stage they have reached in their development, all adolescents in care require special attention. Consequently, we can only endorse the view of Shaw and Hipgrave (1983) that all foster family placements for adolescents, whether they are designated specialist or mainstream, should be 'special' in the sense that they receive the best possible social work input.

Recruiting, training, and valuing foster parents

If all foster family care for adolescents is 'special' because of the complexity of adolescence as a developmental phase, the logical step is to argue that all foster parents who are dealing with adolescents need special preparation for the task in hand. This is the final theme of this book: foster families need training which will equip them for any specialist role they might undertake, including offering some specific form of treatment, helping an adolescent come to terms with the past, improving behaviour and teaching youngsters tangible life skills for independence, to name but a few. Long-term foster families also need specific training to

29

accomplish the demanding task of offering sustained relationships to young people and preparing them for independence.

In addition to training, foster families need to know that agencies value what they have to offer. They need good support systems befitting their role as partners in the care process and they deserve adequate renumeration for their services (Aldgate and Hawley, 1986; Maluccio, Krieger, and Pine, in press). Some time ago, Parker warned us that foster family resources might diminish if we did not consolidate those we had already (Parker, 1978). Recently, the National Foster Care Association has suggested that there is a crisis in London, England, in relation to short-term foster families, who can earn twice as much from daily child minding as they can from fostering. Similar concerns are evident in the US, in the face of the growing attrition and shortage of foster families. We believe that the whole resource implications of these trends should be addressed. If they are not, the whole system may flounder.

With adequate resources, there is room for optimism about the continuing recruitment of foster families. Already in some areas of the UK such as parts of Scotland, mature, able foster parents are being newly recruited from those unemployed in mid-life. In order to recruit more widely, we may also have to be far more sophisticated in our approach than we have been so far. Chapter 9 includes some ideas on how we may proceed. We have to rework our assumptions in relation to the assessment and selection of foster parents for adolescents. These assumptions may be rather different from those which have been applied to younger children. Furthermore, given the widening range of roles and tasks in fostering, social workers may have to make a parallel widening of their criteria for suitable foster parents. Major strides have been made in this area in relation to the recruitment of black foster families for black children; this success gives cause for optimism in other directions.

Most importantly, we have to examine honestly and openly the power relationships in the partnership between foster parents and social workers. Foster parents are currently junior partners in the child care system. This does not prevent them from working successfully within this limitation if roles and activities are scrupulously delineated. But, in the end, if foster parents are to reach their optimal potential, a partnership of equality is the ultimate aim. Some social work agencies have responded to the call for greater equality by changing the name of foster parents to 'community carers' or 'foster care workers'. While this expresses in a tangible way the professionalization of foster care, changing a name is merely window dressing if it is not accompanied by a true change in status demonstrated by training, support, an equal part in decision-making and adequate financial remuneration.

CONCLUSION

Achieving these changes on any large scale demands a radical rethinking in the allocation of resources; but changes are essential if the trend continues towards large numbers of adolescents coming into care, and if foster care is seen as a preferred alternative to residential care for many of these young people. If changes do not occur, we shall continue to see young people leaving care ill-equipped for adult life. Conversely, if the progress which has already been made in many social work agencies is now consolidated and expanded, it might well be possible to report much more positive outcomes within the next few years. Our belief is that social services, both in the UK and the US, owe it to the young people in their care to provide them with the same opportunities for preparation for adult life which are afforded many young people who are fortunate enough to grow up, at their own pace, within their own families.

2 Concepts of parenting and adolescence – implications for fostering adolescents

Tony Hipgrave

INTRODUCTION

Recent years have witnessed a considerable increase in written analyses of the structural components and practice wisdom which make up the complex umbrella term 'fostering' (foster care practice). Within the world of fostering, there has also been a clear growth in the trappings, both organizational and educational, of professionalization. There has been a move towards establishing a disciplined base for fostering (see Chapter 3) but the application of current social science perspectives to this discipline still seems uncertain. This chapter addresses this issue. It deliberately concentrates on the theoretical framework of foster care practice, recognizing the importance of getting this right. There are four main parts: the need for theory development in fostering viewed from the perspective of a social scientist, the concepts of parenting and adolescence and, finally, the application of these two concepts to fostering practice.

THE NEED FOR THEORY DEVELOPMENT IN FOSTERING

The theoretical sub-structure which one might expect to see in informing a truly professional discipline seems to have been slow to develop in literature on fostering. This is, to some degree, understandable. As an applied discipline develops, a valuable first stage in establishing its formal parameters is the description and analysis of the practice wisdom already in existence, and in respect of fostering this process has evidently and rapidly taken off during the last ten years. Most of what is available in the current fostering literature falls into this category, aiming at the development of a practice theory and, in specific areas, for instance in foster parent training and the use of contracts, notable headway is being made (see Chapters 7 and 10).

For fostering, in particular, there are a number of factors which militate against the smooth development from description of practice through definition of implicit practice theory to new theories for practice. First, fostering is commonly practised under pressures which require quick action and decision-making. Second, despite the existence of national bodies, such as the National Foster Care Association in the UK and the Child Welfare League of America and the National Foster Parent Association in the US, the organization of fostering is largely localized so that policies, practices and emphases differ from area to area. Third, universities and other training establishments in the UK have not – unlike the US (see Chapter 10) – played a particularly prominent role in the development of either practice theory or training methods. Fourth, with the exception of the recent initiative from the Department of Health and Social Security on child care research (see Department of Health and Social Security, 1985), there has not been a cohesive approach to research in fostering. In spite of this, generally, no one body is identifiable as the catalyst for devising and coordinating research, although the British Agencies for Adoption and Fostering and the National Foster Care Association have both done a great deal to disseminate ideas and research findings. Fifth, 'theory' is never easy to sell to consumers. Over the years my own discipline, psychology, and social work have had an unhappy tendency to couch 'theory' in complicated systems of thought, often accompanied with florid language and often competing over the same territory with other theories or models. Small wonder that foster parents, whilst being interested in better practice, sometimes appear resistant to theory, as the links between the two are often poorly articulated.

None of the above is intended to suggest that fostering is, or has been, viewed or practised 'atheoretically'. Like most of social work in the UK, at least until the mid-1970s, it has been dominated by a neo-Freudian perspective which seeks to make links between earliest parenting experiences (incorporating as we shall see later a very narrow view of the term 'parenting'), and later behaviours, usually aggressive or sexual, in terms of 'emotional needs' not having been met (see also Chapter 9). The theory and language of this model, particularly perhaps in its relationship to that disparate body of knowledge known as attachment theory, have been criticized by many modern psychologists as being descriptively vague and of poor predictive value (see, for example, Sylva and Lunt, 1982) but are, clearly, still powerful in the world of social work. Only recently has there been any prominence given to explanatory models used in fostering which include other systems of thought, such as a cognitive approach to human development or a social learning theory approach or an ecological perspective (see, for example, Gambrill, 1983; Hudson and Macdonald, 1986; Maluccio, Fein and Olmstead, 1986).

As a social scientist who has been neither a social worker nor a foster parent, I would like to use the rest of this chapter to attempt to illustrate, and hopefully, demystify, the potential liaisons which can be made between the social sciences and fostering practice in respect of adolescents. Although space permits only an overview, I will first look at what a social scientist might have to say about the concept of parenting and then at adolescence as a general developmental phenomenon, with a view to examining the practice implications of these analyses.

PARENTING

The use of the very term 'parenting' or 'parenting plus', as some foster parent training schemes have been called (e.g. Child Welfare League of America, 1975; National Foster Care Association, 1980; see also Chapter 10), indicates a movement away from biological relationship (i.e. parenthood) and, in particular, the mother-child axis, towards concentration on wider systems which exert influence on a child's development. Part of this move entails an understanding that children are not passive recipients of adult behaviour, but are participants in interactional and transactional processes. To put this last point more simply: parents do not simply mould their children – children are concurrently moulding their parents.

Despite these shifts in emphasis, there is still some confusion surrounding the concept. Sometimes it is used in the narrow sense of interactions between parents (birth or substitute) and their charges; on other occasions it can encompass not only wider interpersonal systems of influence, but also understandings derived from the disciplines of sociology and social policy. A further complication is that 'parenting', like many other aspects of human life, is a territory disputed by competing major systems of thought, most notably varieties of psychoanalytic, humanistic and behavioural theories.

Taken at its broadest, the concept of 'parenting' is indeed a confusing one. It encompasses complex separate debates on the relationship between earlier and later experience, the effects of race and gender on opportunities and the effects of social policy on behaviour. Even a simple flow chart exemplifying the influences on parental behaviour would have to include all of the elements described in the diagram below, which demonstrates the complexities of competing influences. A personal biography is ongoing and subject to current feedback; social history and contemporary ideology, as well as an individual's cultural roots, influence both personal inner resources and behaviour, as do other sociological variables such as race and class; people's behaviour may be influenced by lack of skills or knowledge or, alternatively, by beliefs which they hold about that behaviour; under different levels of stress the same individual can behave in different ways.

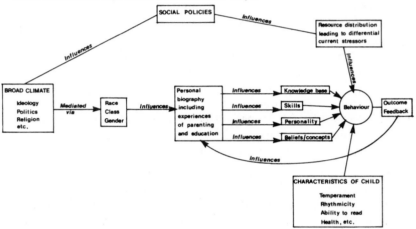

Although the suggestion is not new that the link between social policy and personal psychology merits closer attention (see, for example, Brim and Kagan, 1980), it is small wonder that, when confronted with this level of complexity, people retreat into a narrower focus. Sometimes this retreat is helpful, such as continuing research into the micro-dynamics of parental behaviour (see, for example, Sluckin and Herbert, 1986). At other times, it represents an illegitimate partialization of the picture. It is too simplistic to attribute total blame to parents for their children's difficult behaviour without looking at the influences on parents' behaviour. Similarly, whilst it would no doubt be helpful to include better teaching on parenting skills in the school curriculum for adolescents (see Pugh and De'Ath 1984), to view this as a *solution* is naive, without addressing the issues of the external resources necessary for the proper practice of such skills.

Sometimes, the picture is partialized in other ways. In assessing parental suitability, cultural norms or belief systems are either ignored or addressed ethnocentrically (Ahmed, Cheetham and Small, 1986). On

35

the other hand, purely cultural accounts might be offered (see Ahmed, 1983). Furthermore, personal aspects may be ignored in other ways, such as by offering stress as a total explanation for a particular parental situation, without – for instance – examining skills or knowledge factors adequately, or accounting for the fact that others suffering similar or identical stressors do not react in the same way.

The analytical difficulties inherent in holding together the personal and external dimensions is epitomized in a piece of research by Quinton and Rutter (1984), in which they sought to distinguish the attributes of parents whose children were received into care from a comparison group whose children were not taken into care. Detailed personal histories were gathered, together with data on living circumstances and other potential current stressors. Although the study revealed strong links between parenting problems and disrupted family experiences in the parents' childhood – thus suggesting that current disadvantage cannot on its own be an adequate explanation – there were also striking incidences of severe early adversities in the comparison group, which did not lead directly to current parenting problems. Simple 'continuity' theories cannot thus adequately account for present parenting:

> We must therefore conclude that, when continuities do occur they are mediated by some additional linking mechanisms. Two models for these links have been proposed. On the one hand, continuities have been held to occur through the effects of early disruption on personality development and coping abilities; on the other hand, it has been argued that continuities occur primarily through the trans-mission of material disadvantage, and therefore that disadvantage is a prime cause of family disruption. The findings presented here show that continuities cannot be explained by either model to the exclusion of the other. (Quinton and Rutter, 1984, p. 246)

In other words, parenting is not a unitary phenomenon. It is not an attribute of external circumstances. The effects of parents on a child, or of a child on parents, must be viewed in the context of a family's general material and emotional resources, including, for instance, housing, social supports, demands on time, money and the availability to adults of satisfactions outside parenting. A new, helpful approach is the 'eco-logical' perspective outlined in Chapter 1 (see also Bronfenbrenner, 1979; Germain and Gitterman, 1980; Maluccio, Fein and Olmstead, 1986; Whittaker, Schinke and Gilchrist, 1986). This is based on an understanding of the simultaneous existence and functioning of a multiplicity of systems, both internal and external to a family.

The notion of 'parenting' as a system can be pursued equally profitably in the field of attachments. Although there can be no doubt that positive attachments (meaning relationships which hold emotional significance for a child) are a crucial aspect of a child's development, providing both an impetus to learning and a buffer against setbacks, a good deal of mysticism and confusion surrounds the complex body of knowledge known as attachment theory, emanating largely from the work of Bowlby (1969; 1977). Space does not permit an analysis of a wider debate here (for helpful summaries see Tizard, 1986 and Aldgate, 1988) but the question of attachments is worth pursuing a little in our quest for a better understanding of parenting and its meaning.

It is clear from the plethora of research that has taken place in the 35 years since Bowlby published his original thesis on maternal deprivation (see Bowlby, 1969; 1977) that the phenomenon is different in extent and predictability than was originally suggested. Schaffer and Emerson's (1964) research showed that mothers were not necessarily the primary attachment figures (indeed the very notion of a primary attachment figure is by no means universally accepted) and later research has confirmed that children can have a number of attachment figures, which might serve different purposes for the same child and which might extend outside his or her biological family. Furthermore, attachments are qualitative phenomena and not predictable by the quantity of time spent in interaction or the salience of particular activities (such as feeding). In short, different children develop different attachment systems, both to adults and to other children, to meet their individual developmental demands. New research also suggests that children may recover from severed attachments, given conditions of stability and continuity (Rushton and Treseder, 1986). The relevance of this to our present analysis is that much of what we might conceive as 'parenting' in a functional sense, or as an attempt to 'meet children's needs', might be carried on via several relationships of attachment, so that, when thinking of the parenting which a child receives, or should receive, it may well be necessary to go well outside the birth family or even outside relationships between adults and children. Hartup (1984), for example, has drawn attention to the importance of peers in development. For adolescents, the implications of this might well be that a good deal of 'parenting' is not necessarily done by adults, as the teenage years often bring a shift of some of the parenting functions previously the province of adults towards peers. In assessing the 'fostering needs' of an adolescent, this developmental point, together with others to be mentioned later, should not be lost.

To conclude this attempt to tease out some of the components of parenting, brief mention should perhaps be made of those writers who have tried to attack the question from the angle of 'children's needs' (e.g. Kellmer Pringle 1975 and 1986; Talbot, 1976), or of making prescriptions for good parents (see Brooks, 1981). Both approaches, whilst offering a little light on the subject, suffer from obvious difficulties. Apart from the fact that 'needs' is itself a slippery concept (see Chapter 3), its meaning sliding, often imperceptibly, between notions of necessity, wants and the recipes of 'experts', virtually every list of children's needs applies with equal validity to adults or parents. To borrow from Kellmer Pringle's formulation (1975, pp. 34–38), for instance, parents, too, need love and security, new experiences, praise and recognition, and a sense of responsibility. Indeed, it can be argued, parents deserve to have their situations analysed in these terms, rather than reserving them exclusively for children. The other kind of list – of the 'guidelines for effective parenting' type – tends to suffer from 'overpersonalizing' the concept and reducing it to attributes and skills which float free from a world of competing pressures.

IMPLICATIONS FOR FOSTERING ADOLESCENTS

There are some clear implications in this discussion of parenting for the practice of fostering. Some of the major points are:

1 Any assessment of parenting, be it of birth parents or foster parents, which treats parenting as a simple reflection of personality variables, is to be resisted. Levels of current stress, and family patterns in the face of stress, are an essential part of the picture.
2 Any model used needs to link an understanding of parenting to variables of social policy, race, gender and class. However simple, models, like the diagram on page 35, can act as a check on precipitate analysis and enable a worker to locate the major elements of any assessment or programme. This is particularly important where rehabilitation is a possible goal, in which case it is crucial to know whether a worker's efforts with adolescents and their families should be devoted to skills development, education, the alleviation of stress or the creation of a feedback cycle.
3 Parenting is a dynamic concept. Throughout the childhood years of one child, it may involve a large number of actors. The role of the actors may shift over time so that, for instance, functions which adults

perform for young children may be properly transferred to peers in adolescence. This is part of the general task of retaining a broad developmental perspective, and demands of workers that they are able to define at least the major components of a person's existing parenting system – this may apply as much to parents as to adolescents.

4 A broad systems perspective needs to be developed which can both define the place of previous parenting resources in a current situation and locate the foster family (which could logically take a wide variety of forms) in a 'system of parenting' which is explicitly matched to the requirements of the adolescent, both as an adolescent with common adolescent concerns, and as an individual in his or her own right. Social workers are becoming very skilled in looking at potential foster families systematically (see Chapter 9) – so that, for instance, one of the lessons drawn from specialist schemes for adolescents is the need for a potential foster family to be 'morphogenic', i.e. open in its communication, flexible, enjoying the challenge and having a sense of fun (see Eastman, 1979). The perspective suggested here, however, is wider than that, so that practitioners should not be talking in narrow and individualistic terms about which personality characteristics of these foster parents make them suitable to meet the personality or behavioural deficits of this adolescent, but rather on how the superimposition of this foster family as a system in its own right onto a pre-existing parenting system might usefully meet the physical and psychological requirements of this particular adolescent, and what implications this has for the negotiation of the roles of parties involved in the parenting system. It is not simply a question of replacing one set of parents with another, as Jenkins (1981) has clearly demonstrated, but of reconciling the 'tie that binds' (i.e. birth parents) with the 'tie that bonds' (i.e. foster parents). Similar problems face families who have experienced divorce where children live in one household with one parent and maintain links with the other.

TWO DEVELOPMENTAL ASPECTS OF ADOLESCENCE: IDENTITY AND RESPONSIBILITY

As an age group, adolescents have really captured the post-war imagination and are often treated as a kind of barometer for the general state of a nation's moral fibre or mental health. Thus, the casual reader would not have to wade through many books on the subject, whether novels or of the heavier variety – or newspapers for that matter – to come across one of a number of stereotypes which pervade lay consciousness on the matter. Adolescents are variously portrayed as tortured souls, misunderstood visionaries or malicious victimizers, depending on the perspective of the observer.

In modern Western society, adolescence is a complex and largely artificial phenomenon. It seems to begin with a biological change, puberty, and end via a number of social definitions – for instance, leaving home, leaving school or college or getting married. Psychologically, therefore, the adolescent is having to handle adjustments to both biological and social changes. Broadly speaking, adolescence can be characterized as a period of continuing protection from the full blast of the adult world, on condition that the individual adolescent will progressively display increasing responsibility and independence. On the face of it, and from the adult's perspective, this seems to be a sensible and caring state of affairs, but it should not be forgotten that the adolescent may experience the teenage years as frustrating due to the excessive prohibitions on them in respect of activities in which they clearly have the capacity to engage, particularly sexual activity and paid work. In a number of societies there is no adolescence, or at least it lasts as long as it takes to perform an initiation ceremony which marks the passage from childhood to adulthood. Putting any pain aside, this can make life a lot easier for an individual than a society in which the legal age at which one is treated as an adult shifts confusingly, depending on whether one is involved in crime, schooling, driving, travelling on public transport, going to the cinema, having sex or drinking in a bar.

Another obvious point, but one that is commonly ignored in the literature, is that an individual's experience of adolescence is dependent on a number of other variables, such as historical time, his or her gender, social class, education, race, and which part of which country he or she lives in. So, being an adolescent in 1943 is a different experience, in some respects at least, from being the same age in the hopeful 1960s, which is itself different from today's world of limited job prospects. A sense of future is an important element in identity formation. Similarly, at the same point in time, how one experiences adolescence will be affected by whether one is black or white, male or female, living in the town or country, rich or poor and so on. We should be on guard, therefore, against over-generalizing the adolescent experience or translating experience from one time – such as our own adolescence – into the realms of present-day social realities.

Clearly adolescence is a time of changes, but is it something which is experienced more dramatically – as an inner turmoil, or overwhelming storm and stress? This is a difficult sort of thing to investigate, but in general those psychological studies which have sought to answer such questions by interviewing large numbers of adolescents have failed to substantiate the notion of a turbulent identity crisis. There does not seem to be any real increase in conflict within families at adolescence, and where there is such conflict, problems in communication have usually existed prior to puberty. Adolescents seem – consciously, at least – less preoccupied with deep introspective crises than with more practical matters such as friendships, finding a job and money. It is possible, therefore, for a number of reasons – mass media sensationalism, an over-emphasis on biological or physical issues, over-generalizing from samples of delinquents or the misreading of superficial non-conformity –that the idea of extreme personal crisis in adolescence has been exaggerated. Or, to put the issue in a more mischievous way, adolescence is more of a crisis for those outside it than for those within it.

A 'crisis' in the narrow and more technical sense of personal reevaluation (as used by Erikson, 1968) is a common part of the adolescent experience as an individual learns to inhabit a 'new' body and occupy a more independent position, both towards their family and towards the wider society. It can be misleading, however, to use concepts such as 'identity crisis' as an explanation for particular adolescent behaviour. This locates difficulties within the adolescent and runs the risk of confusing the 'internal' with the 'external' in an overly artificial manner. The commonplace accounts of 'identity-conflict' or 'culture-conflict' in black adolescents in the UK can ignore the fact that no one can develop a sense of self without receiving feedback as to one's value on a scale of 'societal worth' and of real opportunities to compete equally in the world (see Small, 1986; Brummer, 1988). These are not simply intrapsychic phenomena, but exist equally in the 'real' world. This interaction of the external-social with the internal-personal is at the core of a proper understanding of the concept of identity and is consonant with the ecological and competence perspective on human development and functioning outlined in Chapter 1.

Identity is a term which has become common in our everyday speech but when subjected to closer scrutiny becomes increasingly elusive (see Breakwell, 1983; 1986). As a concept, it has been studied from various theoretical perspectives, all of which suggest, in their different ways, that we seem to experience two different kinds of identity – a personal identity, i.e. our 'real' self, and a social identity, i.e. how we behave, or feel forced to behave, in our dealings with others (see also Chapter 4).

When the two kinds of identity are too far out of line we experience some kind of psychological discomfort, which might range from vague unease to a full-blown 'breakdown'.

Our sense of identity can be threatened – whatever our age – from a number of directions. The security that we 'know who we are' can be called into question from either internal or external sources. Examples of internal changes would be illness, disfigurement (say, in a road accident), or rethinking past events. External changes can be social, such as a change in one's membership of groups, moving home or job, or being evaluated in a different way by people significant or powerful in one's life, or material, such as poverty, or nuclear war. Any of these events can lead people to question who they really are, and the evidence on which their sense of self is built.

Clearly adolescents as a group are likely to experience their identity as under threat both from internal biological changes and from changes in their place in the social order. The extent to which an individual feels disturbed by this threat, or behaves radically differently as a result, depends on a number of factors, particularly perhaps on the resources, personal and material, on which he or she is able to draw for support.

Often, writers on adolescence have attempted to make links between identity crisis and behaviour in psychoanalytic terms, emphasising the turbulent effect of sexual urges and the various problems inherent in finding love relationships outside the home. Cognitive approaches – which deal with how a person thinks – are less commonly found, and it may be worth mentioning one or two relevant matters relating to cognitive development in our quest for a clearer understanding of the concept of identity.

Adults' ability to see themselves as others see them is not one which younger children possess. It has been argued that this ability develops around the pubertal years and includes not only the capacity to view oneself 'from the outside', but also to understand certain kinds of abstract concepts such as justice, morality and other values. In other words, adolescents are often able, for the first time, to begin to understand consciously, and deliberately experiment with, the complex social effects of particular behaviours. Another important side-effect of this shift in thinking is the ability of adolescents to locate themselves more accurately in space and time, and thus to construct a considerably more sophisticated autobiography than was previously possible. So, simultaneously, an adolescent might be capable both of rewriting the past and of experimenting with a number of present-day versions of a newly conceived identity. The peer group is a useful source of support in these enterprises (see Berridge and Cleaver, 1987).

The ability to construct a sense of self can create a volatile cocktail, when added to other possible ingredients of contemporary adolescence. A sense of oneself-in-the-future is part of the adult sense of well-being and it could be argued that the sense of future possessed by many of today's adolescents is qualitatively different from that of their adult parents when they were younger. Human beings also prize a sense of consistency and of coherence. The feedback which we receive from the world at large can be confusing and unhelpful in our quest for a comfortable sense of self. In such circumstances, many an adolescent feels compelled to step beyond the 'normal' bounds of adolescent experimentation in order to create a sense of coherence. The sense of a unified self may only be achieved by adopting a negative, deviant or imaginary identity. As Erikson graphically says, 'many a sick or desperate late adolescent, when faced with continuing conflict, would rather be nobody or somebody totally bad, or indeed dead – and this by free choice – than be not-quite-somebody' (Erikson, 1968, p. 176). As well as a sense of identity, adolescents are expected gradually to accept responsibility for their actions. 'Responsibility' should not be confused with the idea of conformity or doing the right thing. We can perhaps define this in terms of two distinct expectations: the expectation that one will make decisions for oneself, and the expectation that one will be accountable for one's actions. Both of these are attributes expected of adults in our society. They are also attributes which parents expect adolescents to acquire. Within an adolescent's family there is a delicate process of renegotiation for all parties at this time which involves devising an appropriate balance, for parents, between being protective and letting go and, for adolescents, between establishing personal autonomy and accepting, to an appropriate degree, the rules made by those more experienced (or often, in reality, more powerful).

Adolescence is a real testing time for the methods by which parents have chosen to exercise their authority. Issues such as style of discipline – whether, for instance, parents have relied on physical discipline, permissiveness, verbal negotiation, or an erratic cocktail of approaches –come sharply into focus in adolescence, when parents may be confronted with a stronger individual who cannot so easily be physically disciplined or out-argued and who may be wanting to engage in activities of which the previously permissive parent does not approve. The less secure or consistent a family's negotiating style has been before adolescence, the less likely it is that an adolescent will be able to hold the tensions inherent in this contradictory balancing act of belonging and separating within that family. Finding appropriate opportunities to enable adolescents to develop a sense of responsibility is a tricky task for any parent and often a frustrating one, but should be as much a part of a foster placement as any other parenting context. Useful guidance on parenting for parents and foster parents on this task comes from Herbert (1987).

IMPLICATIONS FOR FOSTERING ADOLESCENTS

How might such an understanding of the concepts of identity and responsibility be of use in the world of fostering? First, it should be noted that there is a clear contradiction between the developmental tasks of adolescence and the normal course of successful fostering, which would make adolescence a particularly difficult time for anyone to be fostered. If adolescence can be construed as breaking away from a protected existence, then this process is obviously best undertaken from a secure base. If, however, a foster family is, quite rightly, concerned with providing a secure base for an adolescent, this may clash with other developmental tendencies of adolescence, and understandably be resented by the individual concerned. On the other hand, without a secure base, an individual is more likely to experience a less comfortable passage towards adulthood. This makes the definition of the 'parenting' task in foster home care extremely difficult.

A second point is that issues of identity and responsibility are likely to be applicable to most adolescents who are candidates for fostering. To take the issue of responsibility first: as has been pointed out already, the word has two meanings, one to do with taking responsibility and the other with accepting it. During adolescence, people are expected to become responsible in both senses and the aims of a foster placement should include the provision of opportunities to learn both aspects of responsibility. This is particularly true, and difficult, when past experiences may have led individual adolescents to believe that they have no power to make decisions which affect their lives, that other people are always to blame for any trouble the adolescent may be in, or that they always hold the power. Such adolescents are frequently called irresponsible, but often they have not had the opportunity to learn to make decisions and to be accountable for them. Such beliefs as 'others are always responsible for me' or 'I don't have to be accountable to anyone' would need to be challenged within the organization of any foster placement. The placement would need to provide the youngsters with opportunities for taking initiatives, and a system of accountability. It should also offer, or perhaps even demand of adolescents, a genuine role in decision-making. The use of agreements, if handled well, can be an effective vehicle for achieving some of these ends (see Chapter 7).

With respect to identity, the threat to a person's sense of identity, which can be caused simply by being fostered, is compounded by the fact that adolescence in itself is likely to engender a certain amount of instability. This potential double jeopardy needs to be acknowledged and met with a sensitive preparation programme, so that a placement begins with an individual adolescent having some clear understanding of where the present placement fits into a personal past and a personal future. Certainly, within social work an increasing number of tools are being developed which can help towards this end – life story books, geneograms, ecomaps, and games of various sorts (see Laird and Hartman, 1985; Ryan and Walker, 1985; and Aldgate and Simmonds, 1988). In addition, the difficulty which certain groups might have in developing a positive sense of self, by virtue of the social feedback they receive, needs to be acknowledged in the planning of the broader social context of any placement. This is the nub of the debates surrounding transracial placements, as Small (1986) outlines. Additionally, recognition should be given to the fact that continuity with the birth family is a major need for adolescents in care (see Laird, 1979).

A further, and linked, implication from our knowledge of adolescence is that the establishment of a life outside the family is a crucial part of the adolescent experience and also crucial to 'normal' experimentation and the maintenance of a sense of identity. The availability of a community network, including appropriate activities and access to a supportive peer group, should be an important consideration in planning any placement of an adolescent, as should the basic understanding that it is not common for adolescents to share all aspects of their lives and their families.

CONCLUSION

Inevitably, this chapter has been highly selective in its material and arguments. It is to be hoped, however, that the major thrust is clear, namely to highlight the twin dangers of developing practices without reference to wider theoretical bases and of focusing on unnecessarily narrow definitions of parenting and adolescence. A side-effect of such an analysis must be to approach the whole enterprise of fostering adolescents in a critical fashion, and to develop positive arguments in its favour, beyond general statements on the value of family life or community care. The task is not an easy one – this chapter bears witness to its complexity – but is a necessary enterprise as fostering continues to develop as a substantive discipline.

3 Direct work with adolescents – an integrating conceptual map

Masud Hoghughi

The need for a disciplined approach to fostering should not require much arguing. In the last few years, fostering has been through a honeymoon period which may be reaching its end. Many local authorities in the UK set up fostering schemes as cheaper and more acceptable community alternatives to residential placements, sometimes without adequate guidance on policy and practice. As a result, there have been some failures of the type highlighted in the Department of Health and Social Security's study of the boarding out of children (Department of Health and Social Security, 1981), with probably even more damaging results to children than if they had been placed in a group setting.

Even more importantly, there is increasing and wholly welcome demand for open accountability of professional practice, already seen in certain areas, such as in settings where there is a restriction of children's liberty. In the long run, perhaps more important than any of these, is the issue that fostering cannot develop beyond hand-to-mouth pragmatic practice, however good, unless it develops into a disciplined activity which enables that matching of a child with a substitute family environment where, on the one hand, increasingly, the probability of failure is minimized and on the other, the potential for the enhancement of the child is maximized. Social workers dealing with foster home placements must know what they are doing, why they are doing it, and be capable of planning and implementing their actions not only on the basis of clearly articulated concepts, but also of regular, updated monitoring and evidence.

My aim in this chapter is to offer an integrating conceptual map of fostering which sets out its critical elements in a logical order. I use the term 'integrating conceptual map' to denote that I aim to bring together various parts or fragments of fostering; that I am primarily concerned with concepts and ideas from which practices may be generated; and that I wish to offer a route-finding aid.

WHAT DO WE NEED FOR A DISCIPLINE?

A discipline is a systematic, ordered form of intellectual or operational activity such as is seen in philosophy or medicine. It has three basic requirements: ideas, methods and practices.

1 *Ideas* refer to beliefs, values, models and laws which underlie a particular activity. In the present case, fostering itself is an idea with a particular history and points of contact with other ideas about children and what we should do with them. There are a number of models of the functions and purposes of fostering, and information about what types of young people it is appropriate for; these are based on certain values prevailing in our society about the importance of children and the maximization of their welfare, and numerous laws which not only encapsulate many of our most cherished and most important values but also both require and enable us to do certain things concerning children which are legally and financially legitimized.

2 *Methods* are orderly arrangements of the implications of ideas, values, laws, etc. pointing to what should be done. They derive from ideas and lead to practices.

3 *Practices* form the hub of professional activity. Indeed, other than for purely academic reasons, we would not spend any time on the development of the first two dimensions of ideas and methods unless they helped us to perform and develop our practices. Practices are essentially about such matters as who does what, how, with whom, when, based on what evidence, with what expected and real outcomes, and how the outcomes may be used to aid further practice.

Clearly each of the above elements can be set out at numerous levels of complexity or detail, depending on how much information and evidence is available and how much is required to deal with the particular set of circumstances in hand. In medicine, we have extended and well developed varieties of each of the above elements where there is a huge measure of agreement at lay, social and professional levels. In social work generally, and fostering in particular, however, we do not have as much evidence or consensus on any of the three dimensions. The possibility of developing such a consensus will only occur as social work becomes more systematic and self-critical in monitoring its practice. Each of the above three dimensions can be evaluated in such terms as validity, reliability, coherence, usefulness and applicability, but these can be left for detailed exposition at a later stage of development of fostering or foster care practice.

FOSTERING WITHIN SOCIETY'S VALUE SYSTEM

Fostering is a significant form of intervention in children's lives. To justify such intervention in the first place, we must consider the views of society. In the briefest terms, every society's prime task is to survive. To do so, it must set up mechanisms where requirements of order are enforced and opportunities are provided for the achievement of its significant values. 'Order' is about sequence and predictability, 'values' are about things that matter. To achieve these aims of order and value, society sets up a system of social control which has both statutory (formal) and voluntary/non coercive (informal) elements. Social control, defined in these terms, has three objectives. These have been discussed elsewhere (Hoghughi, 1983) and are summarized briefly here:

1 Enhancement of whatever is deemed to be good, desirable and worthy of achievement for its own sake, as seen in such measures as encouraging children's creativity, sporting prowess, and the like.
2 Maintenance of status quo and whatever is deemed either not to need change or to be actively preserved against change, such as religious or political affiliation.
3 Curbing, curtailment and eventual elimination of whatever is deemed to be undesirable, bad and unacceptable, such as ill health, poverty, crime, racial conflict and homelessness.

Fostering is an instance of this last, third, objective. However, in an advanced, multi-value society such as ours, enhancement of the positive potential of the child (objective 1) and protecting him or her against encroachment by others so as to allow his or her normal development (objective 2), are also significant elements. It is, nevertheless, important to emphasize the main objective of controls (i.e. turning something that is unacceptable into something less unacceptable) because social workers and foster parents frequently forget that the basis of their intervention in the young person's life is primarily to ameliorate his or her condition and render it less unacceptable, whether this arises out of being an orphan, neglected, temporarily homeless, delinquent, promiscuous or being unprepared for leaving care. If this is the basis for intervention in young people's lives, who then are the young people who are deemed to require it?

ADOLESCENTS' PROBLEMS AND 'PROBLEM' ADOLESCENTS

Many young people present conditions or behave in ways that we may not like but we put up with them. Almost all young people are ill from time to time, have difficulties at school, throw temper tantrums or engage in anti-social behaviour and have other problems that cause us concern. The reason why we put up with these is that they are within our tolerance level. The behaviour is not so severe or extensive, in relation to the youngster's total condition and our ability to deal with it, that we feel that he or she should be removed from home.

Young people who become the subject of fostering are those whose condition is 'unacceptable' and, because of this, we are moved to do something about them or their condition. This unacceptable condition may take forms such as:

- being physically abused or neglected;
- being mentally handicapped and not receiving adequate care;
- having a seriously unsatisfactory home where the normal require-ments of care and control are not met;
- committing such delinquent acts as to make continued stay at home undesirable;
- being promiscuous or mentally disturbed;
- not receiving adequate care at home.

The common thread in all of these conditions is that they are unacceptable. This 'unacceptable condition' is what we could define as the 'problem'. The young person is not receiving adequate care and control at home. Fostering can be seen therefore as one of the least detrimental ways of providing substitute care and control.

The enormous power of this definition lies in provoking the question 'unacceptable to whom, when, where, etc?' Clearly, what is unaccept-able to one person is not so to another and what is unacceptable under one set of conditions and at a particular time is not so at another. All we have to do is think of sexual behaviour, drinking, smoking and temper tantrums to recognize how our judgements of these actions change with the age and the circumstances of the youngsters involved. This shows that a problem is made up of a 'fact' and a 'judgement' and, whereas the fact may not be disputable, the judgement frequently is. Most parents involved in care proceedings do not dispute the facts of the opposition's case, but rather the interpretation and the judgement based on those facts. The same variations in judgement may well account for quite different rates of populations of children and young people in the care of different social services/social work departments (see Packman, 1986).

CLASSIFICATION OF PROBLEMS

To even talk of a problem suggests the existence of certain criteria and classifications of what is problematic and what is not. We have already looked at the idea that problems can only be sensibly defined as 'unacceptable conditions' allowing for variations in judgement, according to shifts in latitudes of tolerance. More importantly, we need a classification to allow us to look at the totality of young people's problems, making sure that we have not left out anything significant or have not identified them simply on the basis of our own idiosyncratic preferences or preoccupations. Such a classification should be:

- directly usable by both professionals and lay people;
- systematic;
- comprehensive;
- avoiding use of jargon;
- allowing for change in young people or within their circumstances;
- theoretically unbiased; and, above all,
- pointing to appropriate intervention.

However, a classification of young people's problems that takes account of the above criteria has been difficult to find. The affairs of adolescents in care are often divided among various professions, such as medicine, education, social work and psychology, despite a fundamental belief that young people are integrated wholes. In an attempt to bring together these various parts into one classification, the 'problem profile approach' has been developed (Hoghughi, Dobson, Lyons, Muckly and Swainston, 1980).

In explaining this approach, it is first useful to define the terms. 'Problem' is defined as an unacceptable condition; 'profile' encapsulates the idea of change both in the young person and in his or her circumstances, including those who are judging his or her condition. Profiles may change as the young person or circumstances change. Similarly, as the young person changes, develops or responds to help, so his or her problems change. Alternatively, if the person who is judging this condition changes, such as to a tolerant foster parent, so the judgement of the problem changes; the word 'approach' refers to a flexible way of looking at problems and not a theory or a model in the more restricted sense.

The problem profile approach (PPA) divides all the problems that young people present or experience into six areas, which have strong parallels with the ecological approach outlined in Chapter 1. These are:

1 *Physical* – everything wrong with the body and its functions, but including such organic conditions as schizophrenia, epilepsy, addictions, solvent abuse and tattoos;
2 *Cognitive* – everything to do with a young person's problem-solving ability shown in intellectual, educational and vocational spheres;
3 *Home and family* – huge complex of problems from the young person's locality, state of his or her home, and birth status to individual problems of parents and their relationships, the quality of affection, guidance, communication with and control of the young person, the young person's relationships with parents and peers, and attitudes to his or her home;
4 *Social skills* – concerned with a young person's difficulties in making and maintaining socially satisfying relationships with peers and adults;
5 *Anti-social behaviour* – all offences and major rule-breaking behaviours but also disruptiveness, running away and attempted suicide;
6 *Personal problems* – limitations or abnormalities of personality structure – such as extreme extraversion, abnormalities of personality traits such as frustration tolerance and impulsiveness, clinical conditions such as abnormal anxiety and fears, poor moral development and distortions of self-image.

As all children tend to present or experience one or more of these problems at some time, we require some means of distinguishing them from each other. This we do in the following terms:

a) extent – the number and spread of impact of problems;
b) intensity – severity of the problem;
c) duration – how long the problem has shown itself;
d) urgency – the priority that a problem must be given in the treatment of the young person.

Thus, the uniqueness of the young person lies in the cluster and profile of problems he or she presents or experiences. An occasional criticism of this approach is that it emphasizes problems at the expense of the young person's strengths. The reason for this emphasis, as already indicated, lies in a recognition of the 'social control' elements involved, in that it is problems and not strengths which demand intervention. However, the approach recognizes that problems, though the necessary basis for action, require an ecological context if they are to be resolved successfully, including efforts to mobilize the person's actual or potential strengths and resources.

PROBLEMS AND NEEDS

In social work literature generally and fostering literature in particular, the word need is used much more frequently than the word problem, as a basis for action. At its most fundamental, needs arise from the gap between 'what is' and 'what should be'. Need, however, is both philosophically and psychologically a most complex concept. It is an 'inferred' state, i.e. something that we do not see or hear or touch but rather have to deduce from certain behaviours or conditions. We can speak reasonably of a child being breathless after a long run and therefore being 'in need of rest', or a young person saying that he or she is very hungry and therefore 'needs food'. We can make reasonable inferences in these areas because, biologically, human beings are very much like one another; because we know about our own need for rest and food we can extend this to young people. As we go farther away from such physical inferences, we begin to tread on extremely thin ice. Much of what has been said about the needs of adolescents primarily involves adults' interpretations either of requirements of basic decency towards them (arising from our cultural values) or of certain of their physiological states. More importantly, when we say young people need something or other we are justifying doing something to or with them. To this extent 'need' statements are justificatory and should, therefore, be open to public accounting. However, characteristically, these statements say much more about the person who makes them than about their subject. The statements are also usually made by people who find it difficult to justify them statements on the basis of more generally acceptable evidence. Because 'need' statements provide a fuzzy, ambiguous, partial and idiosyncratic basis of intervention, their use in all professional dealings with children and young people should be avoided.

TASKS WITH YOUNG PEOPLE WHO HAVE PROBLEMS

The first part of this chapter has attempted to identify the requirements of a discipline, the basis of intervention (i.e. the relationship between the family and the state), and how we set about identifying adolescents with problems; this part of the chapter outlines the 'conceptual map' of tasks professionals might undertake with these young people. The following diagram represents, in schematic form, the necessary and sufficient actions that must be taken with a youngster who presents or experiences problems:

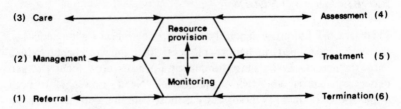

The map sets out the 'critical path' or the logical order of steps that should be taken in dealing comprehensively with every young person who presents or experiences an 'unacceptable' condition and therefore (in the present context) warrants fostering. *Referral* is the point at which an adolescent is identified as being at risk. At this stage, the emphasis is on *Management*. This will include a brief assessment but places the emphasis on curbing and containing the young person's problem condition so that it does not deteriorate. Examples would be an adolescent who has been subjected to sexual abuse and must be protected against further injury or a young person who has committed a serious aggressive act and must be contained and stabilized prior to other steps being taken. *Care* refers to all the actions which must be taken to ensure survival and enhancement of the young person's physical, emotional and social states. Only when these two steps have been adequately taken can we proceed to a fuller and more formal assessment. *Assessment* at this stage is a continuous process of determining a young person's problems and deciding what should be done about them. *Treatment* is concerned with doing everything that is necessary to ameliorate the young person's problem condition as determined through the earlier step. When the problem has been resolved and the basis for intervention no longer exists, intervention is *Terminated*. To undertake any of the above steps demands availability of human and material resources whose use and actions must be monitored to evaluate the outcome of intervention and take whatever other steps are necessary.

The two-way arrows at all significant points of the map show the cyclical and dynamic nature of intervention and the potential for going from any one point to another, depending on the condition of the young person. So, if in the process of discussion with a young person as to why he or she came home late last night (i.e. assessment) the young person takes an epileptic fit, the talking is stopped and action is taken to ensure that the young person does not suffer unduly from his or her fit (management and care). Space precludes detailed elaboration on the implications of the above map or the ideas, methods and practices associated with these steps, but readers might like to refer to Hoghughi *et al.* (1980) for further guidance. Briefly, the map makes it possible to sequence our actions with adolescents in a disciplined way so that we can identify our difficulties both individually and collectively, in order to arrive at a reasonable programme of how we should develop our knowledge and competency in each area.

In this review, there has been an attempt to elaborate four factors:
- the elements of a discipline;
- the broad basis of fostering;
- classification of problems;
- a conceptual map of the tasks that must be undertaken with young people.

These can be placed together to provide a comprehensive representation of these ideas, which could be called a 'universe of discourse'. This involves all the elements of the discipline of fostering and can be represented in diagrammatic form.

The cube below represents, schematically, all the things that we need to know to be able to deal with the problems that a young person is likely to present or experience. What is necessary is to elaborate and set down what we know about the *Theory and Practice* (1), which is based on the underlying discipline of *Ideas, Methods* and *Practices*, in undertaking any of the *Tasks* (2) of management, care, assessment, treatment, monitoring and resource provision relating to every one of the six *Problems* (3). This is clearly a gargantuan task but there is already in existence a great deal of information which we can begin to systematize.

It is helpful to begin by looking more closely at *Theory and Practice*. Although this chapter does not allow the space to say very much about the value dimension, which is an important part of the general concept of theory, it can be assumed to some extent that, as a single, though multi-faceted culture, we share the most significant values about the worth and dignity of an individual and the reasons why we must ameliorate his or her problems and enhance his or her condition. Additionally, ideas and values are encapsulated in our legislation, which both enables and requires that we should take certain actions and thus provides an adequate starting point.

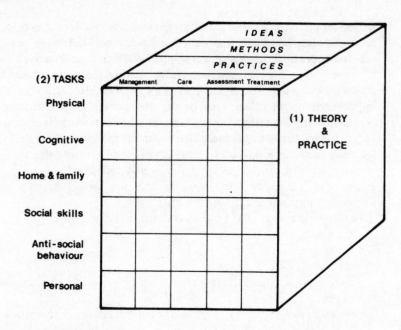

Social work methods are also a part of Theory and Practice. Unfortunately, they have suffered from the same fragmentation as problems, only with a great many more partisan claims for all sorts of peculiar approaches which have been glorified by the name 'method'. In attempting to develop a discipline of treating youngsters with severe problems, my colleagues and I have evolved what we believe to be a comprehensive classification of the major methods which can be used. These have particular relevance for adolescents. These methods can be broadly classified into:

- goods and services delivery – everything to do with the provision of goods and services, such as the provision of a pair of spectacles for an adolescent with poor eyesight or contact with the housing department for a youngster who must get a flat;
- physical – relating primarily to medication and operative surgery;
- behaviour modification – the application of broadly based 'laws' of human learning and unlearning to change behaviour;
- cognitive – using a person's problem-solving ability to deal with a problem, such as remedial education;

- talking therapies – the use of purposive conversation in insight giving and support, as in psychotherapy and counselling;
- group therapies – using group dynamics as a means of changing behaviour, as in family therapy and positive peer culture; and, lastly,
- environmental therapies – harnessing changes in the environment as a medium of changing behaviour, as in therapeutic communities or planned treatment environments. (Hoghughi *et al.* 1985)

What is immediately clear is that none of these methods is pure and, indeed, every one of them contains elements of the others. The classification, however, serves to bring together what we know about particular, systematic ways of helping young people and, to this extent, allows us to build a body of knowledge which can be relatively simply taught for use by anyone who is concerned with problem adolescents.

And what of *Practice*? This dimension contains everything that is done by everybody to help an adolescent with problems. Clearly, it is a huge area, which we are just beginning to analyse and evaluate. Nevertheless, we do know a good deal about every one of the tasks of management, care, assessment and treatment in the different problem areas outlined in the problem profile assessment, which gives us a firmer knowledge base for intervention (see, for example, Hoghughi *et al.* 1985). Here, I believe assessment and treatment warrant special mention, because of their particular position in fostering.

Assessment

This is one of the areas of social work practice about which a great deal is known. Assessment is about finding out what a person's condition is (problems and strengths) and what should be done about it. A number of approaches based, for example, on 'diagnoses' and 'understanding' have been adopted towards it. Given our state of knowledge in social work (outside small areas of physical medicine, education and psychology), it seems likely that the only legitimate approach to assessment is a descriptive one, of which the problem profile approach is an economical example. All assessment is based on information; all information can generally only be acquired from one or more of three sources:

1 Questionnaire data, involving interviews, questionnaires and records of statements;
2 Life data, involving observations, both direct and indirect, structured and otherwise;

3 test data, which include all our tests and measures, concerning every aspect of the child and his or her wider context.

The above sources of information encapsulate most things to which we, either as professionals or as lay people, can have access.

Clearly such information carries different degrees of reliability, validity, utility and relevance, depending on its source and the purpose for which it is required. A considerable amount is known not only about these aspects of the sources of information, but also about pros and cons of particular ways of tapping into them. This is, indeed, the bread and butter of selection psychology, whether it is in education, clinical practice, business or the armed forces. It is extensively written up (e.g. Cronbach and Gleser, 1967; Dorcus and James, 1950; and Horst, 1966) so that social workers and foster parents could adapt these ideas as a means of improving the efficiency of their current practices.

In my knowledge of the practice in the UK, and judging by the literature, interviewing remains the primary medium of gathering information for assessment at present, which generally results in the worker's judgements of the foster parent being presented to a panel of social workers, independent lay people and local politicians. This information then leads to the determination of whether the applicant should be selected as foster parent or not, once certain basic factors such as criminal records and health have been sorted out. Interview, though the most productive, is also the most vulnerable and is often an inefficient source of information gathering, heavily affected by contextual factors such as the conditions under which the interview takes place, and open to bias on such grounds as prejudice against colour of a person's clothing, speech or social manners or because of inherent racism. It is for this reason that there is a need to widen substantially the basis for information. We have recently been working with a special fostering team to try and develop a more widely based and structured process of information gathering. We have developed a number of instruments which are now being incorporated into a new training programme developed by the National Foster Care Association (details available from that organization). All indications are that both the providers and users of information welcome the greater structure that our instruments are providing.

Treatment

I have already indicated that the basis of fostering is that an adolescent is subjected to or presenting an 'unacceptable condition'. Fostering is used as a means of reducing the extent and intensity of that unacceptable condition and bringing it within our society's tolerance. This process of alleviating or remedying a condition so that it is no longer unacceptable is how we define treatment and is, therefore, the focal purpose of all fostering. Whereas management is concerned with the containment of problems here and now, treatment is concerned with long term amelioration.

Treatment is complex in concept and even more so in practice. Its roots go back to the practice of medicine, but the concept is increasingly recognized and used in a wide range of other forms of social intervention. Because treatment has been related to the development of particular provisions, our knowledge of what works and what does not is very patchy. Even so, much is known about treatment of all types of problems, though with variable levels of applicability and effectiveness. It is possible to teach the skills of treatment and develop it as a disciplined activity so that it becomes increasingly relevant to the tasks that foster parents and others involved with difficult adolescents face (see, for example, Hudson and Macdonald, 1986; also Chapter 10).

All treatments should be preceded by a treatment plan which sets out the problems, aim of intervention, priorities, resources required, who should do what, when and how, and how the process is to be monitored. In relation to fostering, I believe no young person should be placed without an explicit plan which states why the child is being placed for fostering, what the foster parents are expected to achieve with the adolescent, over what sort of time span, and how the adolescent's various problems are going to be sorted out, by whom. Written agreements are an integral part of the translation of these plans into practice, as explored in Chapter 7. Both the social worker and the foster parent become not only direct executive treatment agents (in, for example, treating an adolescent's temper tantrums or stealing) but are part of an ecological approach where they also act as co-ordinators of a number of other people's efforts (such as the medical practitioner, the teacher and the youth leader). It makes enormous sense not to put the total burden for the treatment of the young person on the foster parents, knowing as we do that neither they nor anyone else by themselves can deal with the totality and complexity of all the problems that an adolescent presents and experiences.

CONCLUSION

I have only touched on many of the significant issues involved in the practice of fostering, and would not pretend that what I have set out so far will answer all the questions concerning a discipline of fostering. I hope I have done enough, however, to suggest the usefulness of a conceptual map which integrates the major steps that must be taken to turn fostering practice into an increasingly systematic, evidence-based activity. The process of fostering and the critical steps that must be taken in it are not mystical – they can be taught by a few and learned by many, if only we are prepared to put in the necessary work to achieve this end. I believe that we should now go beyond the incantatory enthusiasm which has permeated the recent wave of claims for fostering and begin to look more seriously at how we may improve its practice through intensive, systematic help to social workers involved in fostering and to the foster parents whom they are expected to select, train and support.

I hope this outline provides the ground plan and foundation for building up and developing good fostering practice. Our young people, the foster parents and all of us who care about what happens to them, may deserve much more than this, but they certainly deserve no less.

4 The contribution of young people and their families towards improving foster family care

Jane Aldgate, Mike Stein and Kate Carey

INTRODUCTION

In recent years, problems faced by young people in care generally have gained more publicity. Much of this has come from accounts of care given by consumers of the system (e.g. MacVeigh, 1982; Page and Clarke, 1977; Kahan, 1979; Festinger, 1983; Mann 1984; Lupton 1985/ 6). From 1975 the importance of paying attention to the views of young people in care has been acknowledged in British legislation through the welfare principle (see Chapter 1) which requires that, according to their age and understanding, the wishes and feelings of children in care should be taken into account when professionals are making decisions about their lives. Unfortunately, the reality reported in consumer studies seems rather different from the intentions of policy makers and legislators.

This chapter outlines some of the major areas of concern identified by the main consumers of the foster family care system – the young people and their birth parents. It complements the views of the other main participants in the foster care system – the foster parents and the social workers – which are reported in Chapter 5. The evidence is drawn from accounts given to researchers by young people who were, at the time of their interviews, still in care or were speaking retrospectively, from the standpoint of young adults who had exited from the care system. Supporting evidence is given from others significant in children's networks to argue for changes in the foster family care system. It should be noted that some of the young people whose views are reported here are talking from experience of both foster family care and residential group care, others from residential group care only. Since most studies do not distinguish between young people who have spent many years of their childhood in care and those who have come into care in adolescence, they are a heterogeneous group. This does not invalidate what they have to say, since the principles of involving young people in decision-making and preparation for leaving care still hold, irrespective of the length of time in care or type of placement. Similarly, the views of birth parents, who talk from their experience of dealing with foster families and residential social workers in both long-term and short-term placements, provide ideas on how to improve service delivery in general.

A useful starting point is to look at the complex relationship between the family and the state. Both in the UK and the US, child welfare legislation has developed with the dual aim of protecting children from adults who intend them physical or emotional harm and of offering benign support to families under stress. Sometimes, it seems difficult to reconcile the two without transmitting to children a sense that their families have failed them. Furthermore, while the children themselves may not be directly to blame, they are likely to suffer guilt by association. Consequently, care has often been seen by its recipients as a stigmatizing experience that sets them apart from the general population. This theme is echoed in many of the consumer studies and is well summed up by one respondent: 'When I first went to my school there was some money being pinched and I felt so guilty because I knew I was from a Children's Home and I felt I was picked on, and I knew it wasn't me' (Page and Clarke, 1977, p. 16).

In addition, in both the US and the UK, children from ethnic minority families seem to be even more disadvantaged when exposed to the institutional racism inherent in a 'white', ethnocentric care system. This has been fully discussed elsewhere (Small, 1986), but it is well expressed by one young person at the first 'Black and in Care Conference' held in London, England, in 1985.

> *It is bad for your child to be in care*
> I can't face this life alone.
> Cause I've always lived in a home.
> Thrown out at seventeen
> with no friends or family.
> Thank-you Social Services for your hospitality.
> Here I am in a black community.
> I have grown up 'white' but they can't see.
> Which do I turn to – white or black?
> I daren't step forward, I can't step back.
> Help me someone please
> to find my culture and identity

Why could I not have these when I was young?
They brought me up to think being black
is wrong.
Black people out there
You've got to be aware
For it's bad for your child to be in care.
                    (Quoted in Stein and Carey, 1986, pp. 155–6.)

This poem highlights one important issue for young people in care. There are others, which also deserve attention. What is striking from consumer studies of young people and birth parents is the remarkable consistency of views presented on both sides of the Atlantic. These provide us with clear evidence of major areas for improvement of social work practice and confirm practice areas that are handled well by professionals. It is as useful to report the successes as the failures, to reaffirm that good practice does and can exist. The issues discussed in this chapter are both positive and negative and are necessarily selective. They may be grouped under four areas:

1 The lack of control which some young people in care feel they have over their lives.
2 The effects of disruptive placements on young people's education, social networks and identity.
3 The issue of the maintenance of links with birth parents – its significance for adolescents and difficulties for parents.
4 Preparation for leaving care – consumer views on the effects which lack of preparation may have and recommendations for improvement.

LACK OF CONTROL OVER CARE

In many families, as considered in Chapter 2, the period of adolescence marks a shifting ground in the relationship between parents and young people, with an increase in negotiated decision-making and independence between the two. When young people are placed in foster family care, their parenting is shared by birth parents, their foster parents and their social workers. This 'corporate' parenting diffuses the responsibility between the adults but may lead social workers to be tougher than birth parents on social issues, such as young people staying overnight with friends, because of their sense of public responsibility.

One of the major themes reported by young people who have been in

63

care (Stein and Ellis, 1976; Page and Clarke, 1977; Kahan, 1979; Festinger, 1983; and Stein and Carey, 1986) is the absence of consultation and participation in any major decisions affecting their lives. From their 'Leaving Care' study, Stein and Carey formed a strong impression, particularly from those who entered at an early age, that respondents were the passive recipients of care; they spent most of their lives in care, decisions were taken about them, for them, above them but rarely with them. Some representative comments by young people in the study follow:

'What do you mean by reviews? . . . I don't know . . . I don't think I have. Mum's been to a lot of meetings.'

'No I haven't had one review. I don't even know what they are.'

'Never had a review in me life.'

'I think I did but I didn't really – I didn't really think about them. I know that I've had them but they were nothing to do with me really. I didn't go or anything . . . I never got asked anyway.'
(Stein and Carey, 1986, p. 44).

The views of these young adults are remarkably similar to those in Festinger's study. She reported: 'a recurrent theme in their comments was the importance of consulting with children and allowing them to share in and contribute to, decisions that need to be made'. By the age of ten or the early teens 'children should be able to have a voice in where they are placed . . . if a kid is old enough to be transferred around like a ping-pong ball he is old enough to decide where he is happy . . . children in foster care grow up very quickly.' The young people 'advocated inclusion in decisions about the type of placement, changes in placement, visiting with or return to the biological family, and issues connected with their schooling' (Festinger, 1983, p. 281).

Young people in the above study also suggested they should have more say in the type of homes they were sent to, including the introduction of a trial period in two homes, on the basis of which they might decide which would be preferable. Although, at first sight, this idea might be viewed as totally unrealistic, it should be taken seriously, bearing in mind the constraints of available placements, since research suggests strongly that, if a young person is not emotionally ready to accept the placement, this can be a major cause of foster family home breakdown (Aldgate and Hawley, 1986; Berridge and Cleaver, 1987). With no real control over their lives appropriate to their age, young people are likely to exert what power they do have, even if this is done in a negative way, like running away from a placement or being disruptive at school.

THE EFFECTS OF CHANGES ON YOUNG PEOPLE

Over the last two decades, studies of foster care in general have repeatedly cited breakdown as a major component of foster family placement although, as Shaw (1988) points out, until recently there has been little attempt to address the problem. There are difficulties in defining and measuring breakdown, as Rowe (1987) reminds us. Nevertheless, recent consumer research (Berridge and Cleaver, 1987, Stein and Carey, 1986, Festinger, 1983) reinforces the picture that a most distinctive and distinguishing characteristic of the care experience for young people leaving care is change. In Stein and Carey's *Leaving Care* study (1986), for example, many of the young people had lived in both children's homes and foster care. In the participating sample, just under 40 per cent of those who left care at 18 years of age had experienced five or more different placements and, even in the comparatively shorter term, of those who left care at 16 and 17, 60 per cent had experienced three or more movements in care. For a young person, a change of placement usually meant an abrupt end to care relationships and a sense of failure such as a fostering breakdown or a trial period at home not working out, followed by a changing social world; that is, an adjustment to a new substitute parent or care staff as well as a new neighbourhood, different friends and a new school. It would not be unusual then for a young person to have experienced four or five different surroundings and sets of living companions within their short lives. Berridge and Cleaver (1987) found similar movement among their children in long-term foster care. Similarly, respondents in Festinger's study 'admonished agencies over and over again for moving children around' (Festinger, 1983 p. 275).

Change reported by young people who have been in care is not confined to the moves they make themselves. They may be equally affected by removal of other children from their placement (Festinger, 1983; Stein and Carey, 1986), nor can they always expect stability from social workers. As one young person told Stein and Carey 'I swapped and changed my social worker like I do my socks . . . I just had that many' (Stein and Carey, 1986 p. 44). Certainly, in the minds of both children in care and foster parents, there seems to be an association between social work visits and potential removal of children (Aldgate, 1977; Festinger,

1983). This fear may be justified; changes of social workers can cause a dramatic shift in the care plan, which in turn may cause placement disruption (Aldgate and Hawley, 1986).

The impact of these changes on young people has been well documented by them. One major consequence of placement disruption is the tendency for young people to blame themselves or feel they are responsible for the ending of the placement (Berridge and Cleaver, 1987). Festinger suggests that young people in her study saw movement as 'a punishment for unacceptable behaviour' (Festinger, 1983, p. 276), while the insecurity about movement was prominent among respondents in Thorpe's study, as exemplified by this young person: 'I think you are only out in a certain place for a certain length of time, say two or three years and then you are supposed to be moved. I don't know why –perhaps people get fed up with you' (Thorpe 1980, p. 91).

The full impact of change and the emotional consequences of breaking relationships, from the point of entry to care to the changes within care, have been reported with alarming frequency (e.g. Rest and Watson, 1984; Triseliotis, 1980; Stein and Carey, 1986; Department of Health and Social Security, 1985). The cumulative and negative effects of care are captured by the words of another young person:

> I've got a great big space around me which is mine and nobody enters, and why, I don't know whether it comes from care having been let down so many times, or living with people for so many years and then going, and you never see them again, you build up a barrier in order to protect yourself, which is wrong but you're only human because you get hurt so many times. People try to break it to get in and you don't let them because you're so frightened that it's going to happen again, you're going to get let down or hurt again and that's it with me you see. I mean I don't talk to many people . . . I never get to know people, I think sometimes the reason you never get anybody is because you want somebody so much that you never get them in that sense, what I mean is when you do get to somebody you cling to them so much that you lose them, because they can't cope with the pressure you are applying on them. That comes from having nobody . . . once you've got somebody you think that's it mine now and nobody is going to go near him or her . . . and it's putting pressure on other people that they can't cope with.
>
> (Stein and Carey, 1986, p. 137)

THE EFFECT OF CHANGES – ON EDUCATION

Not surprisingly, any change that occurs in young people's lives, for example the entry to care itself, may bring disruption to the educational progress. As Jackson (1988) identifies, the educational progress of children in care is an area which, until recently, has received little attention either in the UK or the US. Currently, in the UK, the Economic and Science Research Council (ESRC) is promoting initiatives of research into this area (see Aldgate, Colton and Heath, 1987). It is therefore worth noting that a major area of concern for the young people leaving care in Festinger's study was the fact that they felt insufficient priority had been given to their educational progress. There were several problem areas. The first was ensuring that children were helped to value education. The second was the reported expectations from both teachers and workers: 'The social worker gave me the impression I should accept limitations about training . . . just because I had had problems . . . it freaked me out' (Festinger, 1983, p. 277). Some of the young people in this study also recommended that the attitude of the foster family to education should be accounted for when assessing their suitability to foster, and a positive attitude should be favoured. They believed that education should be seen as an important compensatory factor for loss of a birth family. A similar finding was recounted by Triseliotis (1980), who noted a tendency to low aspirations by foster children themselves and their foster parents: 'Compared with their social background and experiences, the children performed as well as could be expected, though education furnished them with very little that might stand them well in adult life' (Triseliotis, 1980, p. 152).

Stein and Carey's respondents also reported very low levels of attainment, with few taking exams at all and not one staying at school after 16. Furthermore, there was little interest in school or school subjects and many saw exams as pointless and education as a whole as a waste of time. There was an exception to this – a remedial unit attached to one assessment centre which provided an informality and closeness to teachers to which the young people responded.

Even if school can be held a constant factor when a young person changes placement while in care, the emotional impact of breaking attachments with significant adults may well take its toll, as one teacher reported about a nine-year-old following a foster home breakdown:

She's a different child completely now than she was before the fostering breakdown, and her emotional insecurity gets in the way of her learning. She was always a popular girl in her class but now she is much more distant in her relationships with her friends as well as with me. I've also found her on her own crying in the playground more than once. She is much less confident about things than she used to be before the recent changes. (Berridge and Cleaver, 1987, p. 165)

THE EFFECT OF CHANGES – ON SOCIAL NETWORKS

Changes in foster homes and changes in schools also have a considerable impact on the disruption of young people's social networks. As suggested in Chapter 2, peer relationships form an important source of stability and provide reinforcement for a developing sense of identity in adolescents. Peer supports come from two main sources – siblings and friends. There is considerable controversy as to whether siblings in care should be placed together but Berridge and Cleaver's study provides some new evidence that, irrespective of the type of foster family placement, placing siblings together can have a positive influence on the outcome of a placement. School friends may also provide support through friendship and give young people opportunities to show off their talent, whether it be, for example, through sports, drama or other group activities which have an element of achievement. The value of peer support is summarized by Berridge and Cleaver.

'Peer support' – for example, from siblings to school friends – which seems to be valuable in helping children cope with adversity; this is also likely to be a benefit in a longer term if such relationships are maintained. It is clear, therefore, that change and uncertainty are more easily managed if they are restricted to specific areas rather than if one's entire social life disintegrates – so often the reality, regrettably, for many children in care and the situation that is often exacerbated by the care process. (Berridge and Cleaver, 1987, p. 185)

THE EFFECT OF CHANGES – ON IDENTITY

The concept of identity has been given prominence in several of the consumer studies on foster care practice and, as suggested in Chapter 2, is a central developmental issue for adolescents.

Triseliotis offers a useful definition of identity embracing three elements:

1 A childhood experience of feeling wanted and loved within a secure environment.
2 Knowledge about one's background and personal history.
3 Experience of being perceived by others as a worthwhile person.

(Triseliotis, 1983, p. 23)

It is perhaps significant that the experiences most highly rated by young people in consumer studies are those where there was a single placement, often with relatives or friends, or a placement which was permanent. In Stein and Carey's (1986) study, a small number of long-term fostering placements also provided some of the closest, warmest and most enduring relationships (see also Triseliotis, 1980). In these situations the young person usually became part of the complete family framework, including taking on foster grandparents, aunts and uncles, best friends and neighbours. Even where young people lost contact with their birth families and their foster families, the importance of belonging to a kinship network was emphasized by the fact that some young people 'adopted' the families of their girlfriends and boyfriends:

'It's a good job I've got his family, I get on great with his family so . . . I go there more than to me own.'

'His mam's really nice, she's great, so I sit in with her sometimes. They've got a big family so it makes up for what I haven't had really, so it's good.'

(Stein and Carey, 1986, p. 111)

For these young people, 'it was not just a case of finding that they could get on with other people's families, but of consciously recognizing the need for a family which would claim them, and which they in turn could claim as their own' (Stein and Carey, 1986, p. 111). Perhaps, as Bush, Gordon and LeBailly (1977) remind us from their study of children aged 10–18 in care in Illinois, (reviewed by Shaw, 1988), there is a simplicity in children's wishes – for love, care and understanding. In the end, these may be the basic qualities required by a young person from any foster family, be it short-term, specialist or long-term.

The yearning for stability and a sense of belonging to a family expressed in the consumer studies adds considerable weight to the permanency planning movement, based on an ecological approach (Maluccio, Fein and Olmstead, 1986) with the dual emphasis on reinforcing young people's existing social networks, including contact with birth families and providing them with one family that becomes a family for life (Triseliotis, 1980; and Thoburn, Murdoch and O'Brien,

1986). Such a recommendation requires a new look at the extended use of the foster family as a permanency planning option (see Chapter 5; and Stein and Carey, 1986).

Triseliotis's second element of identity – knowledge about one's background and personal history – has been the subject of several research studies. Consistently, attention has been drawn to the confusion which young people have experienced in relation to their past, their knowledge of other members of their family, their knowledge of reasons for coming into care and why they are moved in care. This factor was particularly evident in Stein and Carey's (1986) study. The level of knowledge or understanding of those who came into care very young was and, in some cases, remained very low during their whole life in care. They admitted to gaps in memory which were like missing parts of their lives and spoke of partial revelations about their past as 'very disturbing'. Young people who come into care for the first time in adolescence are more fortunate in that they may have a clearer sense of self and knowledge of their personal histories, but even this group may be vulnerable to losing contact with their families of origin. The implications for social work practice are that more thought needs to be put into sustaining links with the past rather than trying to compensate for them.

There has been considerable progress in developments in direct work with children to avoid genealogical bewilderment and to help children who have lost track of who they are or where they have come from to piece together the past and provide themselves with the rationale for rejection (for a recent review of direct work, see Aldgate and Simmonds, 1988). One of the most popular ways of helping young people with identity building is the use of life story books (Aust, 1981; Ryan and Walker, 1985; National Foster Care Association, 1987a).

Finally, within the concept of identity, there is the issue of how young people are seen by others. Festinger's respondents spoke of how they wished to deny they had been fostered children. They, along with other consumers, have consistently argued how the care process itself, with, for example, its emphasis on medical checks performed by strangers, the purchasing of clothes by order forms from one particular shop, the bulk buying of food and the elaborate process of young people gaining permission from social workers to indulge in the normal habit of staying overnight with known friends, contributes to the stigmatization of young people in care (Festinger, 1983; National Association of Young People in Care, 1983; Lupton, 1985/6; Stein and Carey, 1986; Rice and McFadden, 1988).

It has already been suggested that peer groups can be seen as a source of support for young people in care but, in circumstances where a young person is seen as 'different' or as 'an outsider', the same peer group can become punitive and threatening. In such circumstances, as the following account shows, it is hardly surprising that children in care lash out at those who wish to destroy their fragile sense of self and make them feel the 'odd one out':

> 'If you haven't got a mum and dad you're a bastard – you know. And I didn't like that at school. If anybody said that to me I used to bray them.'

> 'All kids started making fun of you, oh where's your mam, where's your dad? And I used to end up in quite a few fights 'cos of that. Oh – she's one of kids' home lassies her, keep away from her she's got nits and things like that. And you'd let it go so far and then you'd lash out at them and then they wondered why you were on report all the time.'
>
> (Stein and Carey 1986, p. 46)

MAINTAINING LINKS WITH BIRTH FAMILIES

There is now considerable evidence from research studies (see Kelly 1986) that children and young people can enhance their sense of identity by maintaining links with their families of origin. Although evidence of the influence on the well being of youngsters of maintaining actual contact is still slightly controversial (Rowe, Cain, Hundleby and Keane, 1984), research has tended to confirm rather than deny its value (Thorpe, 1980; see also Kelly, 1986; and Lake, 1987). There is now a very clear association between rehabilitation and parental contact (Fanshel, 1975; Aldgate, 1980; Millham, Bullock, Hosie and Haak, 1986). There is an even more significant research finding, which relates to young people who are coming into care for the first time in adolescence. It now seems that, on discharge from care at 18, the most likely source of permanence for this group lies with their birth parents (Millham, Bullock, Hosie and Haak, 1986; Thoburn, Murdoch and O'Brien, 1986). Some family relationships may hold a special significance. Stein and Carey found that the closest 'family' relationships that were sustained during the two years after leaving care were those between daughters and mothers and brothers and sisters: 'I always turn to me mam, I mean I know I've got quite a few of me family around me, but I'd be stumped without my mother' (Stein and Carey, 1986, p. 108).

But by no means all the young people in the above study related well to

71

their own families and some had deliberately severed contact with them. The difficulties of maintaining contact with birth parents have been well documented (White, 1981). In White's study, young people themselves had much to say about visiting. For example, they stated that visits from parents brought out painful feelings about the reality of their situation and about separation and loss, and that they did not get enough help to deal with these feelings. Therefore, some refused visits, and some were physically afraid of their parents. One youngster reported that she always brought a friend along on visits home as a protective measure. Others felt that visiting activities and schedules were arranged to meet the needs of the two sets of parents and not their needs. On balance, however, the young people, the two sets of parents and the social workers all agreed that the long-term benefits of visiting outweighed the immediate problems. Some benefits mentioned were the lessening of the need to suppress separation feelings and to engage in fantasy (idealizing the good and exaggerating the bad); and increasing opportunities for parents and young people to nurture developmentally appropriate relationships.

Parents of children in care have also identified the benefits and difficulties inherent in maintaining contact with their children in foster care (see particularly Family Rights Group, 1986; Gibson and Parsloe, 1984; Kelly, 1986; Maluccio and Sinanoglu, 1981, all of which give useful summaries of research findings and practice implications).

Reviewing the major research findings, there are seven factors which may be of considerable significance for the maintenance of contacts between parents and young people in foster family care:

- the impact on parents of filial deprivation;
- self-motivation of parents;
- the encouragement of social workers;
- the positive attitudes of family and community;
- the positive attitudes of carers towards birth parents;
- the positive attitudes of young people towards their parents;
- the nearness of the placement to the birth family home.

The impact which separation can have on parents, filial deprivation, is well known (Jenkins and Norman, 1972; Aldgate, 1980). These feelings are summarized by a birth parent: 'The fact that you are visiting your child in a foster home is a reminder that you are, at least for the time being, a failure as a parent. You are very sensitive especially during the first visits' (McAdams, 1981, p. 309).

The implications for practice from the filial deprivation studies are twofold. First, parents are under stress at the point of entry to care and need help in their own right at this time. Secondly, parental separation experiences may be an important factor in predicting which families are likely to maintain contact with their children easily and which need a great deal of encouragement (see Jenkins and Norman, 1972).

A second factor influencing parental contact relates to parents' belief in the value of maintaining links with their children. These parents are more likely to continue to see their youngsters than those who believe that it is best to leave their children alone while they are in care (Aldgate, 1977).

The third, and arguably the most important, factor is that parental views on the value of visiting may be modified considerably by social work encouragement, as this father in one study describes:

Miss McKinnon came round to see why I hadn't been up to see the children. I told her that they were awfully upset when I went so I didn't think it was a good thing to go again. She told me that this would pass and they needed me to visit or else they would be even more upset. She was right but I don't think I would have gone back if she hadn't taken the trouble to come and fetch me.

(Aldgate 1977, p. 421)

Fourth, if there is an expectation from families and friends that parents will maintain links, the moral pressure exerted may urge them to keep in touch whereas the birth parent who is isolated from kin and friendship and who lacks a community support system may be likely to stop visiting (Kelly, 1986). A good example of the influence of family on parents also comes from Aldgate's study:

When my sister and her husband (in the army) came home from overseas and found I had put the children into care she was that mad she took me up to the social workers straight away and it wasn't long before they were home again. I'd never had done it on my own.

(Aldgate 1977 p. 423)

Fifth, the attitude of caregivers towards parents may also influence the contact they maintain with their young people in care. Burch, writing from the perspective of a foster parent, believes that foster parents can themselves do much to encourage parents.

When parents become disheartened or disillusioned and fail to make contact with their child a letter from the foster parent reassuring them of their welcome in the foster home and of their child's need for them – accompanied by a photograph of their child – will often bring a positive response. Such a letter should always be sent with the social worker's knowledge and agreement and a copy may be considered necessary for the file. Birth parents should be given every chance to work towards reuniting their family. They should not be left to feel that no-one cared, no-one understood, no-one helped or showed them how.

(Burch 1986, p. 118)

Alongside their attitudes, the arrangements caregivers provide for birth parents and adolescents to meet during visits are also highly relevant. As one mother described to Aldgate (1977):

You feel like you're intruding, as if you don't belong there and your children don't belong to you. I never know what to say when I go there. You're expected to sit down and talk to the children. I can't talk to them. I talk to Mrs Anderson [foster mother] instead.

(Aldgate 1977, p. 446)

Sixth, parents may be discouraged when their children react to parental visits with indifference or anger, because of their feelings about being in care. Young people themselves have reported that the rift with their parents may sometimes be so great that they prefer to maintain a degree of distance and not to seek help or support from their families for fear of being further excluded (Stein and Carey, 1986).

Finally, there are the practicalities of maintaining links between parents and children. The distance between the parental home and the foster home presents a major obstacle in many cases. Children placed within their own community are far more advantaged (Kelly, 1986). Additionally, links have been maintained most successfully where young people have been able to return to the parental home for visits or have been able to use homes of extended family members as a facilitating base (Aldgate, 1977).

Consumer studies have much to tell us about the barriers which may prevent parents from maintaining contact with their youngsters in care. The way forward is to identify the attitudes, setting and content of meetings which will provide a supportive structure for everyone concerned. Some ways of doing this are explored further in Chapter 6.

PREPARATION FOR LEAVING CARE

Maintaining links between parents and young people in care may be one way of providing a support system for them which will help ease the transition out of care and the establishment into adult life (Maluccio, Krieger and Pine, in press). Where support from birth families is not available, extended support from foster families or from other community-based families known to young people may be equally valuable. The studies discussed in this chapter once again emphasize the need for a shift from the use of the term 'independent' living to 'interdependent' living (see Stone, 1987; also Chapters 1 and 5).

In the UK, research studies have also questioned the wisdom of the independence approach. The notion of complete independence is, in effect, expecting young people who have experienced difficulties in past relationships and whose current family relationships may be stressful, broken or missing to achieve a level of skills and maturity ahead of their peers from 'ordinary' backgrounds (Stein and Carey, 1986; Lupton, 1985/6).

If social work agencies are serious about offering a supportive framework to young people in care that is relative to the transition period for many young people not in care, then they need to explore the range of opportunities for extended support until young people are 'ready' to move on (which may be when they are in their early twenties).

The research also poses other questions about the independence approach. In their training programmes, 'independence units' tend to become over-preoccupied with practical skills and downgrade the significance of relationship skills. Furthermore, Stein and Carey's (1986) study led to the conclusion that, such is the power of the ideology of independence, that a 'preparation for independence' unit in the local neighbourhood is sometimes likely to cause dislocation rather than investment in locality. What seems to happen to many young people who have been in care is that their care experience swings them sharply from dependency to an expectation of independence. Many react by moving in with other people – by moving to 'interdependence'. In Chapter 8, this theme is taken further by looking at the provision of supportive programmes for interdependent living which offer a combination of nurturing relationships and appropriate housing or other accommodation.

Finally, the consumer research concerned specifically with leaving care, both in the UK and the US, has necessarily thrown up many questions about the management of care in itself. Stein and Carey (1986) provide a comprehensive evaluation of resource and practice areas which need to be improved. These include fewer changes in care, the greater participation of young people in acquiring tangible life skills (see also Chapter 6), exploring the possibilities of maintaining stronger links with families and neighbours during care, offering extended support beyond care (see also Chapter 5), paying greater attention to the education of young people in care so that they may have equal opportunities for employment and, finally, recognizing young people's vulnerability to homelessness.

The major problem remains – what happens to young people when they leave care? Perhaps more thought needs to be given to the whole question of what might or should constitute the sustained relationships for young people in care which would provide continuity during and after leaving care. This opens up the whole question of maintaining links with kin and community whilst young people are in care, alongside a rethinking about how family or residential care may be extended to provide interdependent living which, in turn, will ease the transition into adulthood.

5 *Preparation of adolescents for life after foster care*

Miriam Kluger, Anthony Maluccio and Edith Fein

As considered in Chapter 1, both in the United Kingdom and the United States a growing proportion of young people in foster family care are adolescents. Some of these youngsters may be in placements which have been defined as specialist (see Shaw and Hipgrave, 1983), but others are likely to be in more traditional long-term fostering, where foster parents are offering themselves as parenting figures to supplement totally or complement in part the role played by birth parents. As the age of majority approaches, these young people face the conflicts and turmoil of all adolescents, but also the additional realities that living in foster care imposes. These include: coming to terms with a personal history different from the norms that society defines; relating to diverse families (foster families, birth parents, and possibly adoptive parents); and preparing for independence from public support at a time when youngsters living with their own families may not need to attain financial independence so quickly.

This chapter poses and attempts to answer the following questions: How prepared are adolescents for life after foster care? What roles can their birth families play in relation to this task? Can their foster families be continuing resources for them? And, finally, is long-term foster family care a viable permanency planning option for certain adolescents within the definition outlined in Chapter 1? The chapter considers these questions by drawing from an extensive US study of children and young people in long-term foster family care in the state of Connecticut, as well as from selected findings from related research. It presents the view of the adults concerned, particularly the foster parents and the social workers, thereby attempting to complement the views of young people and their families outlined in Chapter 4.

THE CONNECTICUT STUDY

The use of foster family care as a permanency planning option has been controversial, particularly since there has been little information on the youngsters, how they differ from those who successfully move out of care, and how they function while in placement. The study on which this chapter is based was designed to be responsive to those concerns (for further details see Kluger, Fein, Maluccio and Taylor, 1986). The research focused on children and young people who were in long-term foster family care, defined as a minimum of two years or longer, although, as will be shown, well over two-thirds had been in their current placement for more than five years and a majority had spent a substantial period of their childhood in foster family care. Its major purpose was to understand the characteristics, functioning, and needs of the youngsters, their birth and foster families.

The study was conducted in the context of a public children's services agency and within the framework of its regular services delivery. This statewide agency has statutory responsibility for providing services to children and youth referred to it because of abuse or neglect, juvenile delinquency, mental illness or other family problems.

The study consisted of an investigation of all 779 children and youth in long-term foster family care in the state of Connecticut on 1 January 1985, thus making it one of the largest studies of foster care undertaken in the US. A major strength was its use of an entire population, thus eliminating sampling errors and providing a large number of subjects for sub-group comparisons. Data was gathered from the state's computerized information system, telephone interviews with the children's state social workers, and in person or telephone interviews with the foster parents. Information was gathered on the child's and family's characteristics, the placement history, the permanent plan, the child's present functioning, and the expectations and plans for the future.

Findings considered in this chapter pertain to the 307 (39 per cent) of the study population who were 16 to 20 years old. Although in Connecticut youngsters normally leave care at age 18, some continue to be financially supported by the state agency until age 21, if they are in college or in some special education program.

Table 1: *Characteristics of children and youth in long-term foster family care*

Characteristics	% of 16 to 20-year-olds (n=307)	% of 2 to 15-year-olds (n=472)
Sex		
Male	47	54
Female	53	46
	100	100
Race/ethnicity[a]		
White	59	47
Black	37	41
Hispanic	4	12
	100	100
Time in foster care[a]		
<3 years	11	31
4–5 years	17	27
6–10 years	19	23
>10 years	53	19
	100	100
Time with current foster family[a]		
<2 years	34	35
2–5 years	26	39
>5 years	40	26
	100	100
Age at entry[a]	7.5 years old	4.1 years old
Number of placements		
1 or 2	66	70
>2	34	30
	100	100
Reason for entry into care[a]		
Neglect	59	64
Abuse	8	13
Other (e.g., economic/environmental, family interaction problems)	33	22
	100	99[b]

[a] Statistically significant difference at the .01 level.
[b] Percentage does not total 100 due to rounding.

CHARACTERISTICS OF ADOLESCENTS AND THEIR FAMILIES

Young people

Part of this study involved tracing the changes in characteristics of young people who came into public care over a decade ago. It has done this by comparing a group of young people, at the time of the study 16 to 20 years old, of whom half were aged 18 to 20, with a second group who were 2 to 15 years old at the time of the study. As seen in Table 1, the results indicate that in some respects there are changes taking place in the types of children coming into foster family care, but in other ways the children are quite similar.

There were similar numbers of males and females in each group, and both groups had approximately the same number of placements during their time in care. Compared to the younger children, however, the 16 to 20 year olds were more likely to be white and to have entered care because of economic/environmental and family interaction problems rather than defined abuse or neglect. It is not clear why there are fewer minority children in the older group. As for the differences in reasons for placement, it is apparent that, in recent years, more younger children have been placed because of the increased recognition and reporting of child abuse and neglect. In addition, youngsters in the older group had spent more years in foster care and with their current foster family and had entered care at an older age. Nearly all 16 to 20 year olds were placed in a same-race foster family. Almost one-quarter were living with a sibling.

Using scales developed in an earlier study (Fein, Maluccio, Hamilton and Ward 1983), the foster youth were assessed by their foster parents in four major areas: school functioning; behavioural functioning; emotional and developmental functioning and foster family adjustment. The average scores for the four scales were at least 3.7 out of a possible 5. Scores were lowest in emotional and developmental functioning and highest in adjustment to the foster family.

75 per cent of the foster parents also considered their foster youth's behavior good or excellent compared with peers. This occurred in spite of the fact that half the youngsters had changed schools – always a stressful event at any time and especially for young people in foster homes. About one-third, however, were attending special education classes or schools.

Birth families

Approximately half of the birth parents were currently receiving services from public or voluntary agencies, including income maintenance, individual or group counseling, or treatment in a substance abuse program. One-third of the parents were in need of additional services of the same kind. Moreover, on the basis of information provided by both social workers and foster parents, at least one-quarter of the parents had a substance abuse problem.

For those 16- to 20-year-olds about whom the social workers had this information, almost all had at least one birth parent living, and half had two parents living. Parental rights had been legally terminated for 19 per cent, and for two-thirds of that group it had occurred more than five years earlier. Fewer than half the parents telephoned, wrote, or sent gifts; only one-quarter of the youngsters had seen their parents three or more times in the past; approximately half the youngsters had not visited with their parents at all.

Foster parents indicated that nearly half the adolescents had negative feelings toward their birth parents, one-third had positive feelings, and one-fifth had no feelings at all. They also thought that slightly more than half would object to being adopted, and that only a few of the youth expected to be returning home soon.

Foster families

The foster parents were a mature group, on average between 45 and 54 years of age; 62 per cent were white, 37 per cent black, and 1 per cent hispanic, a racial distribution similar to the youths'; two-thirds were married; and two-thirds had at least a high school diploma. Half were employed, 10 per cent retired, and 40 per cent unemployed. Poverty was prevalent, since one-fifth of the foster parents reported family incomes below $10,000, and half reported incomes under $20,000 at the time when the official US poverty level for a family of four was $10,989. About half the homes were in urban areas.

The foster parents had an average of two children living in the home, including the foster youth. They were an experienced group, averaging 13 years as foster parents and caring for an average of 17 children during that period. They were also connected to the community, one-third belonging to at least one group or club and two-thirds being active in their religious affiliation. In addition, the foster parents demonstrated an attachment to the youth in their care. Most (88 per cent) said the

81

youngster was the type of child they had originally wanted to care for; 92 per cent preferred that the youth stay in the current home even if another placement were available; and half had considered adopting the child at one time or another. Nearly one-quarter had known the child prior to placement, suggesting an important resource for social workers searching for a foster home for a youth.

PREPARATION FOR SELF-SUFFICIENCY

As adolescents in care approach the age when they will be on their own, preparation for life after foster care and eventual self-sufficiency becomes a major concern. As a result, as described in Chapter 8, agencies are giving increasing attention to independent living programmes (Stone, 1987).

In this study there were differences in the perceptions of the social workers and foster parents about the preparation of youth for independence; social workers felt that one-half of the youth were prepared, whereas foster parents felt that only one-third were prepared. Those 16- to 20-year-olds considered prepared for emancipation by their foster parents had higher levels of self-esteem, and were more sociable, open, and mature, and less rebellious than the unprepared adolescents. The foster parents of those considered better prepared said they had helped by teaching the adolescent about reality and responsibility, setting realistic expectations; budgeting, and other activities of daily living, such as how to cook or shop.

For the two-thirds of adolescents whom they did not consider prepared for self-sufficiency, foster parents identified a range of needs. Over two-thirds of 'unprepared' adolescents needed job skill training and help with planning a budget, handling money, and finding housing. Additional needs reported for at least half the adolescents included parenting skills; obtaining income assistance; finding a job; and maintaining a household. Other needs mentioned by foster parents were: learning how to shop; help with social skills; finding mental health services; sex education; finding recreation services; and using public transportation.

The social workers' reports were similar to those of the foster parents, although, in nearly all areas, social workers perceived relatively greater needs on the part of the youth. Sex education, in particular, was identified by two-thirds of the social workers compared to one-third of the foster parents. This probably reflects social workers' concerns about the increasing problems of teenage pregnancy and AIDS. Another need noted in a number of cases by social workers, but not by foster parents, was counseling to gain more psychological and emotional stability. In essence, foster parents and social workers agreed that adolescents in care have a variety of needs in tangible as well as intangible areas of life skills.

This is not surprising, as the needs identified above are typical of adolescents in general. Moreover, these findings are consistent with other reports (Pasztor, Clarren, Timberlake and Bayless, 1986; Timberlake and Verdieck, 1987), as well as the self-perceptions of former foster adolescents (Festinger, 1983; Stein and Carey, 1986).

Because of their particular status and vulnerability, adolescents in foster care need a range of services and supports if they are to have an opportunity to grow into competent adults. There follows a consideration of what part both birth parents and foster parents can play, particularly as continuing resources for young people after they have reached the age of majority.

Role of birth family

The role of the birth family or members of the extended family has long been neglected in foster care of adolescents. In this study, for example, it is noteworthy that there was regular adolescent-parent contact only in a small number of cases. Similar findings have been reported by other researchers (Hess, 1987; and Rowe, Cain, Hundleby and Keane, 1984). In their British study of long-term foster care, Rowe and her colleagues found that only one-fifth of the youngsters 'had had even casual contact with a parent during the previous year'. As a result, these authors concluded: 'The most remarkable fact about our study of children's family contact is the lack of it' (Rowe, Hundleby, Cain and Keane, 1984, p. 95).

In contrast to these findings, it has been established that the birth family continues to have crucial significance for the adolescent in care, as discussed in Chapters 1 and 6. Moreover, it has been found that many adolescents return to their birth families after leaving care, or at least resume their relationship with their parents or other family members (Jones, 1983; see also Chapter 4).

There should therefore be more extensive consideration of birth families as potential resources for adolescents, during the placement as well as following discharge. The practice of separating young people from their families must be questioned (Lake, 1987). As Loppnow has indicated, 'current knowledge suggests rather that young people need help differentiating from the troubling aspects of their heritage, [while] remaining connected in whatever ways possible to those biological figures central to their identity and experience' (Loppnow, 1983, p. 531).

Social workers, foster parents and others working with adolescents should consider more explicitly whether birth parents can become at least partial resources for their children. This, however, is something that should begin long before the young person leaves care. In addition, parents as well as adolescents require help to develop the skills that may be useful in learning or relearning to relate to each other. Although the parents may not have been competent in bringing up their children, it may be that they can be helped to learn the skills required to relate to them as young adults.

In this regard, both the youth and parents may need assistance, since so many of the parents have serious difficulties like substance abuse and mental illness, and many of the youth have special problems. Also, there are important implications for preventive work with these youngsters, in light of the evidence that a large number of children of alcoholics become addicted (Armor, Polick and Stambul, 1976).

The foster family as a continuing resource

The study suggests that most foster parents develop a strong commitment to the young people in their care. As indicated earlier, nearly half the foster parents had considered adopting the youngster, and most expected the youth to remain in the home until the age of majority.

In addition, other studies have shown that, after leaving care, adolescents often remain connected to their foster family and return to it in times of crisis (Jones and Moses, 1984). Yet, currently, the young person's relation with the foster family is officially terminated when he or she is discharged from care, and payments to foster families are ended. These actions imply that the foster parents' involvement is no longer needed or valued, since the youth is now expected to be independent.

It is true that young people in care, as with adolescents in general, struggle to become emancipated from parent figures, including their foster parents. But this does not mean that they do not have a need for linkages with a family. On the contrary, in at least some situations, the foster family can be a source of ongoing support and connectedness. The continuing importance of a particular foster family for each youth should therefore be explored and reinforced to maximize connections whenever possible (Maluccio, Krieger and Pine, in press).

Having such expectations of foster parents also means that agencies need to consider providing incentives and supports to the foster parents even after the adolescent officially leaves care. In light of the poor economic situation of many foster families of adolescents, this should include some form of continued financial support to the foster parents.

The findings of this study suggest, as did those from the *Leaving Care* study reported in the previous chapter (Stein and Carey, 1986), that there is a very strong case for formally extending official foster care placements beyond the age of majority to allow for the transitional period into independence. We can only emphasize that it is becoming increasingly unacceptable to expect young people, who are by definition ill- prepared for adulthood, to cope with circumstances that would not be expected from the substantial majority of their peers living with their birth families. The resource implications are obvious but if public service care truly wishes to perform its parenting function to the best of its ability, these dilemmas have to be addressed.

LONG-TERM FOSTER FAMILY CARE AS A PERMANENCY PLANNING OPTION

A further question that arises from the study is whether long-term foster care is a viable permanency planning option for some adolescents. This question has long been debated, in part because of research findings documenting the drift of children in foster care (Maas and Engler, 1959; Rowe and Lambert, 1973; Rowe, Cain, Hundleby and Keane, 1984) and the number of placement breakdowns (Berridge and Cleaver, 1987; and Proch and Taber, 1985). Should the field continue to place negative value on long-term foster care, in comparison to adoption or reunification of children with their birth families?

As considered in Chapter 1 this study suggests that the time has come to develop a more positive attitude towards long-term foster family care. One of the most prominent findings was the stability of foster care placements for most young people; two-thirds of them had had only one or two placements, and half had spent more than three-quarters of their time in foster care with the current family. There was also evidence that children did not remain in foster family care indefinitely on an unplanned basis but that there was identification of a permanent plan for nearly every youngster, with foster family care as a preferred option in many cases, but eventual adoption by foster families being the ultimate aim in almost one-quarter. Moreover, there was indication of positive functioning for most children and of the foster parents' expectation that most youngsters would remain with them until independence.

The implications of the study are that a foster family can offer stability and be seen as a preferred option on a planned basis for some young people. Therefore, in conjunction with research which has questioned the supposed damaging impact of growing up in foster care (Festinger, 1983; Maluccio and Fein, 1985), these results lead to the need to rethink the issue of foster family care as a viable permanent plan, especially in circumstances of children for whom reunification or adoption is not appropriate. This conclusion is also supported by the findings of Thoburn, Murdoch and O'Brien (1986), who describe foster family placement as one of the valid 'routes to permanence' and remind us that, for older children, adoption is not always an appropriate alternative to reunification.

The research by Thoburn and her colleagues (1986), along with that of Rowe and her colleagues (1984) and Triseliotis (1980), has attempted to identify the circumstances in which long-term fostering may be appropriate, and leads to cautious optimism. Further research is needed. There should be, in particular, attention paid to questions such as: which youngsters need and might profit from placement in long-term foster family care; which services and processes should be stressed to promote the functioning of adolescents in care; and which safeguards should be required to ensure stability and permanency. In addition, there should be a detailed examination of the needs and situations of the one-third of the youngsters with multiple placements, for whom foster care currently does not provide stable living arrangements. As shown by a recent demonstration project, it is possible to increase placement stability for those adolescents, through intensive services, careful case planning, and comprehensive supports (Taber and Proch, 1987).

CONCLUSION

The developmental tasks of adolescence present hurdles for all youth and their parents. The youngsters who grow up away from their birth families face particular difficulties. In addition to the typical tasks of adolescence, young persons in foster care face a variety of unique challenges, including coping with the impact of separation from their birth families; making peace with the birth family; and establishing connections with other significant figures in their social environment without the usual family supports.

The findings of this study suggest that, where permanence cannot be defined in terms of reunification or adoption, long-term foster family care can be an appropriate permanency planning option to help some adolescents deal with these challenges. A variety of services and supports is required, however, to assure that the emotional growth, maturity, and adjustment of adolescents are optimized. Benign outcomes for future generations depend on our ability to accept the implications for resource development and provide the needed services for all participants in the drama of foster family placement.

6 Intervention with adolescents in foster family care and their families

Inger P. Davis

This chapter is set within the ecological perspective which, as described in Chapter 1, emphasizes the use of intervention for the purpose of strengthening the supportiveness of the client's environment as well as the client's competence in dealing with all the components of that environment, through the acquisition of specific skills (Germain and Gitterman, 1980; Maluccio, 1981). It also means willingness and ability to blend professional interventions with various degrees of social networking through the multiple roles of treatment agent, teacher, counselor, broker, advocate and network consultant (Whittaker, Schinke and Gilchrist, 1986).

The focus in the chapter is on ways in which adolescents in foster family care may be helped. Attention is paid to the maintenance of ties with the birth family, the development of social skills, and social work intervention aimed at helping address behavioral, cognitive or emotional problems and the aftermath of separation and maltreatment. Although the emphasis is on the roles of social workers, the roles of foster parents are fundamental to the success of intervention, as discussed in Chapter 10.

THE FOSTER ADOLESCENT'S TIES TO THE BIRTH FAMILY

Parental involvement

Parental involvement with young people before, during and after placement is a crucial component of permanency planning (see Chapters 1 and 4). To promote such involvement, writers such as Blumenthal and Weinberg (1984), Gambrill and Stein (1985), Horejsi, Bertsche and

Clark (1981), Maluccio and Sinanoglu (1981), Maluccio (1985), Family Rights Group (1986) and Lake (1987) stress the following themes:

- making clear agreements with parents, preferably through written contracts with clear objectives and ongoing feedback about changes;
- providing parents with handbooks spelling out their rights and responsibilities;
- regular conferences with parents;
- promoting and arranging parent-child visits;
- providing such services as parent education, self-help groups, counseling, parent aides, financial/legal/vocational counseling, substance abuse programs, joint conferences between parents, foster parents and the child regarding clothing, recreation, chores, discipline, etc.;
- including parents in birthday and holiday celebrations;
- holding internal or external reviews of case plans;
- facilitating parent participation in planning discharge or alternative long-term out-of-home care;
- confronting biases against parents as being 'bad' for having a child in care;
- balancing the focus on parental psychopathology with greater attention to strengths and environmental stresses impinging on the parents' ability to care for their children.

Visiting between the adolescent and the birth family is of special importance for the well-being of the adolescent as well as the parents, as demonstrated not only by attachment theory but also by empirical research (see for example Family Rights Group, 1986).

Attachment theory asserts that stable 'affectional' bonds between parenting figures and children throughout childhood contribute to the well-being of both parents and children. As outlined in Chapter 2, attachment is an interactive process. There is also considerable room for diversity in attachment patterns (Aldgate, 1988). Unplanned, 'unwilling' separations will affect a young person's sense of stability and, if not dealt with appropriately, may cause emotional damage. It is, however, often the circumstances surrounding separation rather than the separation itself which can harm a child or young person more, as studies of children in hospital (Stacey, Dearden, Pil, and Robinson, 1970) and in care (Berridge and Cleaver, 1987; Stein and Carey, 1986) have shown. Parental involvement can reduce anxiety and ameliorate the situation. It is for this reason that, in out-of-home placements, parental visitation is considered necessary to reduce the sense of abandonment and restore self-esteem to both young people and parents. Visitation frees energy for young people to engage in developmental tasks and for them to build nurturant relationships with foster parents.

As suggested in Chapter 4, in relation to children in out-of-home placements in general, empirical findings demonstrate an association between frequency of parental visiting and early discharge, children's emotional well-being, developmental progress and prevention of foster home breakdown (Aldgate, 1980; Thorpe, 1980; Berridge and Cleaver, 1987; Fanshel, 1975; Lake, 1987; Millham, Bullock, Hosie, and Haak, 1986; Rowe and Lambert, 1973). Apart from being an aid to re-unification, there are three circumstances, where adoption is not seen as an appropriate permanency planning option, where the importance of parent-child attachment and parental visiting is clear:

1 the parents have regularly visited the child and the child would benefit from continuance of the relationship;
2 the child is aged 12 or older and does not wish to have the relationship with his or her parents legally severed; and,
3 the foster parents are unwilling to adopt, but the child would suffer if removed from their custody and placed for adoption.

(Barth and Berry, 1987, p. 72)

While the case for maintaining visits between parents and children may be compelling, as discussed in Chapter 4, there are many potential intervening variables which may get in the way of successful outcomes such as 'parental motivation and responsibility; nature of the preplacement parent-child relationship; age of child; caseworker attitudes and specific interventions related to visits; visit length, location and nature of supervision; and nature of the parent-child interactions during the visit' (Hess, 1987, p. 43).

Given the significance of parental child visiting for everyone concerned, it is clear that an explicit agency policy is called for, spelling out details about visits, rights and responsibilities of all parties involved, perhaps establishing a separate record of visits and their content and consequences so as to individualize and maximize the benefits of visiting. (For a detailed exposition of these services, see Reeves, 1986.) The practitioner needs to generate input from the foster adolescent, the two sets of parents and relevant others in clarifying the purposes, expectations and practicalities of visiting; determining when monitoring of visits is necessary; helping the parties get psychologically ready; and giving feedback and offering counseling regarding interactive events occurring during the visit. The preparations may also include structuring activities and content to be discussed during visits.

Blumenthal and Weinberg (1984) present a list of parent-child activities during visits that relate to the adolescent's development tasks and changes. For example, the capacity for abstract thinking, emerging in early adolescence, makes politics, religion, and planning for the future appropriate topics for discussion. Bodily changes call for talks about personal grooming; changes in peer association call for inclusion of the foster adolescent's friends in visitation. Parental responses to the increasing need for independence from parents may include helping the youngster to drive a car, or helping the late adolescent to plan for and actually move into independent living quarters. Some parents have limited understanding of what to expect from their children at different stages of development and need guidance and information in this area. Whatever assistance is given to make visits beneficial, activities must obviously be planned and conducted with sensitivity to the needs and circumstances of the individual case, and to cultural norms and ethnic customs for family interaction.

Given the dearth of material on the management of parental child visiting, it is heartening to hear the major initiative being developed in the UK, as a joint enterprise by British Agencies for Adoption and Fostering, National Foster Care Association, Family Rights Group, the Dartington Research Group and Barnardo's. A working party, chaired by Jane Rowe, is developing a training pack on access and family links for children and young people in care. At the time of writing, details are available from any of the organizations mentioned. The pack is based on the Department of Health and Social Security's code of practice in relation to access of parents to their children in care (Department of Health and Social Security, 1983). It will consist of nine two-hour modules with an optional extension for each, covering topics such as the purpose of access, maintaining access with extended family, making agreements about access, assessing children's feelings and attachments, knowledge of the law and appeals procedures, making decisions about access when children are in permanent placements and dealing with access over time – sustaining links, working out roles and dealing with potential problems. Each session will consist of exercises designed to help people to examine and reflect on their own attitudes and values, to look critically at the policies and practice of their agency and to develop their skills.

While social workers have a major role to play in promoting parent/ child contact, foster parents themselves can substantially affect parents' responses (Aldgate, 1977). An experienced foster mother writes about the responsibilities which foster parents have towards children, young people and their birth parents. Although she is talking about children in general, her ideas are equally applicable to adolescents. Foster parents' responsibilities, she believes, should be agreed in advance with the social worker and should include the following:

- to discuss all aspects of the placement with the social worker
- to set goals for the parents, answer questions honestly, and inform them of changes in their child's [youngster's] routine
- to arrange good contact between parents and child, and help parents demonstrate their motivation and commitment to their child
- to help parents understand their child's [youngster's] behaviour. For instance, a child will sometimes go out . . . while a parent is visiting, knowing that the parent will still be there on his or her return. Parents often feel that this an indication, not of trust, but of the child's not caring whether or not they visit . . .
- to accept other members of the family who may wish to visit, such as grandparents, aunts and cousins
- to help parents understand how others see them and interpret their actions or failure to act
- to accompany parents to court, family planning clinics, open night at school, and the like
- to be involved in reviews and case conferences and give evidence in court
- to offer practical help such as the loan of bedding when a child [youngster] goes home for days and overnight stays, or send food for these stays or help parents buy it
- to help the child to understand why he or she is in care – through play therapy and by making a life-story book or helping parents make one for their child.

(Burch, 1986, pp. 116–17)

Apart from these general responsibilities, Burch also believes that parents may be involved with their children in specific ways. Although she is talking about children in general, some activities are particularly relevant to the maintenance of the relationship between adolescents and parents, such as:

- preparing a meal for the child [youngster] . . . ;
- taking their child [youngster] to the shops . . . , clinic or doctors;
- cleaning their child's [youngster's] room, making the bed, washing and ironing clothes;

- . . . helping the child [youngster] read or write . . . [and other educational matters];
- shopping for shoes and clothes with the foster parent or, better still, going unaccompanied unless they have demonstrated that they cannot spend . . . money wisely . . .

(Burch, 1986, pp. 117–18)

This list is by no means exhaustive. Other activities which reflect the nature of the relationship between parents and adolescents can be developed equally successfully, such as watching or participating in sports.

Furthermore, there are occasions when the parents of young people in care need special attention and nurturing in their own right. Lee and Park give detailed guidance on how foster parents may extend nurturing to birth parents and believe that 'acceptance and respect can be a strong force in the process of building their self-esteem and competence' (Lee and Park, 1980, p. 25). Additionally, it is well known that many parents of young people in care do not have good support networks and are often very isolated. Foster parents may well have a role to become part of the support system to the birth parents (see Sinanoglu and Maluccio, 1981). Programs of respite care currently under way in the UK and the US have drawn heavily upon this principle.

Lee and Park draw on the work of Evelyn Felker, a foster parent, who suggests a number of ways through which foster parents may help birth parents:

1 by supporting the efforts of the parent to be a parent;
2 by playing second fiddle to the child's own parents;
3 by not playing games – in other words by not allowing the foster parents to be placed in the middle of a disagreement between parents and the social worker;
4 by being honest with the parents;
5 by supporting the social worker-parent relationship;
6 by not overreacting to criticism from the parent;

(Lee and Park, 1980, pp. 26–9)

Recently, an effective way of helping parents improve their self-image and parenting skills has been seen in the development of group work with birth parents. In the UK, the National Society for the Prevention of Cruelty to Children (NSPCC), for example, is currently running groups on parenting skills in some of its regional offices. Monaco and Thoburn (1987) report on the effective use of self-help groups for parents. The primary aims of these groups are to give information and advice to consumers, to provide services such as babysitting, to provide social contacts and to invite members to become part of parental pressure groups. The effectiveness of parents' actions within pressure groups is demonstrated by the achievements of the Family Rights Group and development of organizations such as Parent Aid, which has produced an excellent guide for families with children in care. (Bennett, 1987).

Success in involving the birth parents will demand a partnership from social workers and foster parents which is set in the context of high trust between all parties. To further this trust, the use of written agreements (see Chapter 7) is held to be an effective way of reinforcing positive verbal exchanges which have been made between all parties.

Sibling relationships

The practice principle of securing continuity of relationships should not be limited to the parent-child relationship or to maintaining preplacement psychological ties with other significant adults. Siblings often represent an important support system that should be kept alive during placement, and encouraged to continue beyond placement as a network from the adolescent's own generation. Even with the best of efforts, sibling groups are often scattered at placement time into separate homes and with separate social workers. Sibling deprivation is frequently deeply felt by foster children (Berridge and Cleaver, 1987). In a study by Zimmerman (1982) young adults reported that, regardless of the length of time in care, siblings were the persons they wished they had seen more of while in care. Timberlake and Hamlin (1982) urge that, whether all or some of the siblings are being placed, a meeting with the sibling group be arranged as soon as possible to discuss and express commonly held fears that somehow the placement could have been prevented, work on immediate problems, encourage a realistic view of the situation, and make plans for visiting and communication.

A short-term, five-step model of sibling therapy for foster youngsters designed to maintain and develop the sibling network is described by Lewis (1986). The therapist takes a directive stance by becoming the central figure in the first, often chaotic meeting of siblings who sometimes have not seen one another for a long time. In organizing the activities, resolving conflicts, etc., the therapist in the role of matchmaker then guides the children in communicating and relating to one another. As soon as the interaction sustains itself, the therapist moves out from center, and, if a leader is still necessary, helps the 'parental' child become the leader with ongoing coaching from the therapist.

Lewis (1986) illustrates the above approach by a case example of four siblings between five and twelve years of age who were in three different foster homes. Five-year-old Suzi was about to go into a psychiatric hospital because of suicidal and withdrawn behavior. She was staring into space, talking to herself, unaware of the presence of others. Her siblings, with the help of the therapists, were able to pull her out of her isolation, and her behavior in the foster home changed sufficiently to avoid hospitalization. At follow-up several months later the therapist learned that 12-year-old Meg maintained contact with Suzi and was trying to arrange a holiday get-together with her siblings. Lewis concludes that, despite the numerous and time-consuming tasks of arranging schedules and transportation, sibling therapy is one sensible way of not only providing the children with some measure of consistency and continuity, but helping to keep lines of communication open between the many partners and parents involved.

LIFE SKILLS TRAINING AND COUNSELING

Methods for the acquisition of life skills are extremely important for adolescents in general, and essential for foster adolescents because their conflict-filled childhoods have often lacked adequate role models and left many of them with a shaky self-esteem and social skills deficits. The foster family itself is the primary remedial resource in this respect, but the placing agency carries responsibility for providing additional, formal life skills counseling.

In his review of empirical and practice literature, LeCroy (1982) defines one of the life skills, social skill, as 'a complex set of skills which allow the adolescent the ability to successfully mediate interactions between peers, parents, teachers, and other adults' (p. 92), and social skills training (SST) as 'treatment procedures designed to develop and facilitate prosocial responses as opposed to emphasizing the elimination of excessive antisocial behavior' (p. 92). An implicit assumption of SST is that as prosocial behavior increases, antisocial behavior decreases. The procedures used include:

- modelling;
- roleplay;
- feedback;

- prompting certain behaviors such as more eye contact, slower or louder speech;
- selection of goals; and
- behavioral assignments.

LeCroy's examples of behaviors to be mastered through social skills development include juvenile delinquency, aggression and anger in psychiatric adolescent patients, and emotional disturbances. SST has also been used for the purpose of pregnancy prevention and assertiveness training.

In addition to social skills development, Schinke and Gilchrist (1984) apply the life skill counseling model to coping with sexuality; managing stress; promoting health (nutrition and exercise, substance use and abuse); and anticipating employment (career choice, training, job hunting). Euster, Ward, Varner, and Euster (1984) apply a life skills group approach specifically to adolescents in foster care. Their training covers issues in foster care, making friends, information about sex, sexuality, personal and relationship problem-solving, and drug and alcohol abuse. In particular, it highlights the following practice principles:

- need for stability and security;
- avoidance of demands for self-disclosure;
- provision of activities that allow the foster teens to choose their own level of participation;
- responding to sensitive issues;
- selecting activities appropriate to the group's stage of development (pre-affiliation, power and control, intimacy, differentiation, separation).

In life skills groups for young people in care, the differing needs of early, as opposed to late, adolescence must also be considered. The content and structure of discussions about sexual behavior, for example, would vary accordingly. Groups of older adolescents are often more responsive if composed of about equal numbers of members of both sexes, in contrast to early adolescents (12–15 years) who seem to do better if grouped with members of their own sex (see Levine, 1979, pp. 14–15).

Peer counseling programs may serve somewhat similar purposes for adolescents as life skills groups. It is not known to what extent this practice has been tested in foster care; undoubtedly many foster adolescents have been referred to peer counseling in school, religious and recreational programs. While the idea seems viable, 'careful planning is called for, especially since peer-counseling programs in general have had uneven success' (Garbarino, Schellenbach, and Sebes, 1986, pp. 270–271).

SOCIAL WORK INTERVENTIONS

Child welfare agencies, directly or through referral, have experimented with various individual, group and family unit therapeutic approaches to help foster adolescents with emotional and/or behavioral problems that call for more intensive treatment than discussed so far in this chapter. Regrettably only a very small proportion of what is learned from these applications is recorded and shared through published reports. A few examples follow.

One of the most important social work interventions in relation to foster family placement for adolescents is the preparation of young people for placements. This may be done individually (see, for example, Fahlberg, 1981; National Foster Care Association, 1987a; Aldgate and Simmonds, 1988). To this end, the development of 'bridge families' to help children come to terms with past and prepare for future has been effective (Barnardo's 1983). Alternatively, Triseliotis (1988) reports on the effectiveness of group preparation of adolescents for placements.

Timberlake and Verdieck distinguish between reactive and proactive casework needed by older foster adolescents. Reactive casework is designed to help 'resolve residual developmental conflicts and problems as a prelude to dealing with problems of current life transition' (Timberlake and Verdieck, 1987, p. 221). In contrast, proactive casework is focused on enhancing growth and development by helping foster adolescents improve day-to-day functioning; cope with the issues of identity versus role conflict; and begin to confront emancipation issues. The latter approach appears to have much in common with the life skills counseling model discussed above. Both may be successfully used concurrently within a placement program of direct work (Aldgate and Simmonds, 1988).

For mentally retarded foster adolescents Rosenberg (1985) suggests an individual counseling approach, while Lee (1977) describes group work with this client population. Lee and Park (1978) also favor group treatment for depressed foster adolescent girls. Cordell, Nathan and Krymow (1985) discuss format, issues and activities of group counseling of youngsters adopted at older ages. The shared adoptive experience generated spontaneous, consistent and genuine rapport and support in these groups, the benefits of which are reflected in comments such as: 'Being adopted isn't so bad – it has its pluses and minuses', and, 'There are people around you who know what you feel and feel like you do' (Cordell, Nathan, and Krymow 1985, p. 123). Similar groups may prove equally beneficial to adolescents who share the experience of permanent foster care or long-term foster care.

These observations are congruent with those gained from treatment of post-traumatic stress disorder (PTSD). According to Scurfield (1985) many clinicians consider group treatment to be the modality of choice for those who suffer this delayed onset of symptoms and reactions to past traumatic events. As foster adolescents are confronted with identity and other developmental issues, they may also experience delayed reactions to the childhood traumas associated with bringing them into foster care.

Findings of a recent study of the dynamics of adolescent depression by Simons and Miller (1987) confirm that the three factors operating in depressions of adults, negative beliefs about self, feelings of powerlessness and a pessimistic outlook on future educational and occupational opportunities, do not have the same impact on adolescents. The strongest predictors of adolescent depression were a negative view of self, low parental support, and employment problems. Thus treatment cannot be limited to cognitive therapy, which may suffice for adults, but must be supplemented with efforts to change the family environment and counseling regarding employment matters.

A useful technique in working with adolescents is 'network therapy', especially in situations involving suicide crisis, psychosis, drug abuse and other acting-out behaviors (Schoenfeld, 1984; and Speck and Speck, 1985). It involves bringing together groups of 40–50 persons from the adolescent's networks of close family, friends, relatives, neighbors, clergy and others, and it is generally used only after simpler forms of interventions have failed. The invited members meet with the professional network team for several two-and-a-half to three hour sessions to explore new ways of thinking about the problem and to give concrete and psychological support to the adolescents and the family. While professional counseling frequently continues after the network sessions, the ultimate purpose is to shift responsibility from the professionals back to the networks.

Network therapy is not without its critics. Questions about its costliness and practicality come readily to mind. Sprecht, acknowledging that network therapy may be a good idea, finds that so far there is no 'evidence of the utility of drawing squadrons of others into the treatment process. The over-intrusiveness into a client's life (albeit some clients may enjoy the attention) and the costs of this mode of intervention have yet to be justified' (Specht, 1986, p. 233). Nonetheless network therapy is included here as one potential resource. After all, child welfare practitioners, while not using the particular terminology, may in fact be employing this technique in limited fashion as the foster adolescent, the birth and foster families, teachers and others occasionally are brought together for joint conferences.

Practice with foster adolescents also needs to take into account that the impact of separation on the parent-adolescent relationship is especially complicated when maltreatment is the major reason for placement. The affectionate bond, or whatever threads are left of it, must be therapeutically attended to before the adolescent can accept and utilize the nurturance that the foster family has to offer. The psychological wounds of maltreatment are not likely to heal by themselves. At times post-traumatic reactions lie dormant until triggered, perhaps by the placement itself, or by adolescent development tasks.

We are only at the beginning of formulating principles of helping maltreated adolescents in foster care (McFadden, in press). It is difficult to piece together the existing literature. Clinical accounts are scattered throughout the psychotherapy literature in general, and in the growing body of writings on abused and neglected children. In the USA, these sources, however, appear to be focused on the children and young people who remain in their homes, and to some extent on the youngsters who have been seriously hurt to the point of needing hospitalization or other institutional care. The middle group of maltreated children who did not exhibit extreme behavioral responses to the abuse, but still are at sufficiently high risk to be placed in care, is to a large extent overlooked in the literature.

Consideration of practice with maltreated adolescents in general may add to our understanding of the treatment needs of maltreated adolescents in foster care (see for example, Mouzakitis and Varghese, 1985). The strong feelings aroused by parental abuse often add vehemence to the already lively debate over pros and cons of individual, group, and family unit therapy and counseling. Thus, practice principles may be premature, if not hazardous, to formulate. Still it appears that group therapy is generally the preferred modality, particularly for sexually abused adolescents. Most writers also agree that group therapy needs to be combined with individual therapy, either concurrently with, or before and/or after group therapy. Almost all recognize the need for involvement of the victim's family members in treatment; disagreement centres around how they should be involved. Some think therapy with the family as a unit is the only way disfunctional relationships can be changed. Others view family unit therapy as a perpetuation of the abuse in pushing the adolescent further into the grip of the family power structure.

Many factors enter into the difficult choice of intervention modality, such as whether the abuse is longstanding or emerged at adolescence; the level of functioning and internal and external resources of the family; and the degree of impact on, and impairment of specific areas of the adolescent victim's psycho-social functioning.

Some references relevant to the treatment of maltreated adolescents include: Blick and Porter (1982); Boatman, Borkan and Schetky (1981); Borkman (1984); Finkelhor and Browne (1985); Garbarino, Guttman, and Seeley (1986); Mouzakitis (1984); and Porter, Blick and Sgroi (1982). Guerney's (1986) ecologically oriented overview of interventions with maltreated adolescents is particularly relevant for many foster adolescents.

Recently, in the UK, there has been a growth of training literature which addresses the problem of offering help to adolescents who have been subjected to sexual abuse (see, for example, National Foster Care Association, 1987b; Barnardo's 1983). Foster parents have a primary role to play in these treatment programs but need training to undertake their role (see Chapter 10).

With reference to other relevant interventions, interested practitioners may want to consult these references on group treatment of adolescents in general: Berkowitz (1987); Raubolt (1983); and Scheidlinger (1985). An overview of family, group and individual interactions with adolescents and their families is also presented by Davis (1985). The same topics are addressed in Herbert (1987) and Jones and Pritchard (1980). Additionally, there are special problems which demand a specific approach. Dealing with violence or anger in adolescents, for example, is a problem which is at once common and at the same time difficult to handle. Hudson and Macdonald (1986) provide a useful review of literature in this area.

CONCLUSION

In ecologically-oriented child welfare practice, the social worker has not only the responsibility of building a working and sometimes a therapeutic alliance to him/herself but also to 'massage' and influence the foster care and other collaborative systems in a manner that makes it possible for the adolescent and the birth family to form a working alliance with the agency or system as a whole. In addition, the social worker is responsible for contributing to the empirical foundations of practice, going beyond mere counting of adolescents moving in and out of care, and generating data that help us determine which practices and interventions, by whom, when and with whom are most likely to promote healthy development of adolescents in care. Such a contribution is essential to develop improved methods of helping adolescents in care.

7   The use of agreements in foster family placements

Anthony Maluccio and Mike Simm

Over the last decade the service agreement or contract has become a basic feature of social work practice, and its use has been explored by many writers in both the UK and the US (see, for example, Brady, 1982; Corden and Preston-Shoot, 1987; Rojek and Collins, 1987; and Seabury, 1979 and 1985). In particular, consensus has evolved that the agreement can be valuable in work with young people coming to the attention of child care agencies as well as their parents.

This chapter examines the use of agreements with adolescents in foster family care and their biological and foster parents. First, there is a review of the use of agreements in social work practice in general, covering definition and purposes, content, rationale, characteristics, and limitations. Second, there is consideration of principles and issues in using agreements specifically with adolescents in foster care and their families; and, finally, the application of agreements in practice is illustrated through case examples and through material newly developed by the National Foster Care Association in the UK.

AGREEMENTS IN SOCIAL WORK PRACTICE

Definition, purposes, and content

In social work the contract has been defined as 'the explicit agreement between the worker and the client concerning the target problems, the goals and strategies of social work intervention, and the roles and tasks of the participants' (Maluccio and Marlow, 1974, p. 30). The agreement is intended to provide a base for open and honest communication between family members and practitioners. It is not a legal document, and it should not be used to engender an adversarial relationship.

The agreement is an integral part of the helping process in diverse practice settings. In this regard, it is helpful to view it not simply as a product or event, but as a dynamic *process* of engaging clients in examining, understanding, and dealing with their problems or needs. It may well be that the central value of the agreement lies in the process of arriving at a certain formulation, more than the formulation itself. For example, in work with parents who feel helpless, hopeless, and worthless, helping them to make decisions regarding their children's care can be a powerful way of conveying respect for them, aiding them to gain some sense of control over their lives, enhancing their competence, and empowering them even in small measure (Maluccio, 1981).

The agreement can thus serve a variety of purposes including:

– promoting decision-making on the part of social workers, parents, children, and other collaborating persons or agencies;
– facilitating participation of parents and children and thereby promoting their sense of competence and control;
– ensuring clarity of tasks, goals, and purpose for clients, workers, and others;
– specifying time frames for accomplishment of tasks and goals;
– holding all parties accountable and spelling out sanctions or consequences if any party does not follow through with agreed-upon tasks or activities;
– providing for periodic review and assessment of progress.
                    (Maluccio, Fein, and Olmstead, 1986, pp. 121–2)

Many variations of the agreement may be considered to achieve its purposes. These include:

– a preliminary statement focusing on general or broad themes and formulated early in the contract with clients;
– a more definitive agreement reached after adequate discussion and review with clients and others who may be involved;
– a partial agreement delineating in further detail a section of a more general agreement;
– a behavioral contract spelling out the tasks of children, parents, or social workers in dealing with a specific issue or behavioral problem;
– a secondary or supplementary contract between biological parents and foster parents, or parents and other service providers, or child and teacher, among others.

Whichever type is used, in general it seems best to write an agreement, rather than rely on oral discussion. Writing an agreement serves to emphasise its importance, promote clarity, and provide a vehicle for monitoring and reviewing progress (Brady, 1982; Seabury, 1985). It can help ensure that a client's best interests are pursued vigorously and systematically. At the same time, it is essential to guard against using written agreements that are too mechanistic, overly legalistic, or impractical with certain clients, such as those with limited education. (For detailed discussion of writing an agreement in child care practice see Maluccio, Fein and Olmstead, 1986, pp. 120–40).

The content of each agreement varies, in accordance with its purpose as well as factors such as the particular agency and needs and circumstances of the client. At a minimum, however, the agreement should incorporate the following:

– names and identification of all participants;
– explicit formulation of goals;
– specific delineation of roles and tasks of each participant;
– time frames for implementation of tasks and accomplishment of goals;
– arrangements for progress reviews;
– appropriate signatures and dates.

Rationale

The value of using agreements, particularly with children and families, is supported not only by practice wisdom but also by various theoretical and research perspectives.

There is, first of all, the ecological perspective. Its essence is that there is a dynamic interaction between people and their environments, and that the functioning of human beings is strongly influenced by the quality of this interaction; human behavior or functioning is dependent on the *goodness of fit* between (1) the needs and qualities of the person and (2) the qualities of the impinging environment (Germain and Gitterman, 1980). The written agreement can help in identifying and planning for the environmental supports and resources required by clients to promote their functioning.

Second, there is the competence orientation, whose key premise is that human beings are naturally motivated toward health, growth, and competent functioning (Maluccio, 1981). The agreement can be a tool for involving clients in decision-making and goal planning, using their cognitive powers, taking action on their behalf, and ultimately promoting their competence.

Third, the permanency planning movement also supports the use of agreements. Permanency planning is the process of ensuring that children grow up in a family setting, preferably their own (Maluccio, Fein, and Olmstead, 1986). It involves the provision of preventive as well as rehabilitative services, and it relies on the multiple efforts of family members, agencies and practitioners. The agreement can help facilitate permanency planning, through such means as emphasis on clarification of goals, tasks, roles and responsibilities of all participants.

Fourth, there is considerable evidence from various studies and demonstration projects that the structure and clarity inherent in agreements result in prevention of out-of-home placement, reuniting children more quickly with their families, or accomplishing other permanency plans such as adoption (Stein, Gambrill and Wiltse, 1978; Stein and Rzepnicki, 1983).

In short, there is a strong rationale from theory and research for the use of agreements. In addition, there is an ethical dimension: through the process of negotiating an agreement, social workers can help ensure that clients are involved in making and implementing decisions affecting their lives.

Characteristics

For maximum effectiveness, agreements should embody characteristics such as the following as much as possible:

- mutuality;
- explicitness;
- honesty;
- realism;
- flexibility;
- responsiveness.

Mutuality Agreement among all parties is essential, particularly in respect to goals, roles, tasks, and responsibilities. In practice, it is often difficult to achieve this ideal; but it is something toward which workers should consistently strive, especially since research shows that discrepancies or clashes between clients and workers lead to corrupt or covert contracts, double agendas, mutual frustrations and ultimately failure to achieve desired goals (Maluccio and Marlow, 1974, p. 30; Maluccio, 1979; Mayer and Timms, 1970).

The ideal of mutuality requires that social workers and clients form a therapeutic alliance. Doing so with adolescents and parents involved in foster family care can be especially problematic; partly because of their prior experiences with other helping agents or authority figures, they often perceive social workers as adversaries rather than allies. Workers need to be aware of family members' concerns and help elicit their feelings and fears and prior experiences with other workers. Above all, they can relate to the parents' concerns about their child's growth and development and generate the conviction that a child needs and is entitled to permanency in his or her life.

Explicitness Explicitness means being specific, clear, and open. An agreement should be stated in explicit language that facilitates understanding on the part of everyone concerned. Technical language should be avoided. Specific goals and tasks that are pertinent to the needs of the clients should be incorporated, rather than goals that are too global or not relevant.

Honesty In the process of negotiating an agreement, workers should be honest and open with clients. In child care settings especially, clients often do not trust – or have no reason to trust – agencies, workers, or other authority figures. By being honest about their roles and responsibilities, workers can help build the clients' trust in them and in the negotiating process. Towards this end, workers can help by recognizing clients' fears and concerns; bringing out differences in views; and acknowledging the authority of the worker or agency (Hutchison, 1987).

Realism An agreement should be realistic, which means that 'the terms that are agreed on are within the capacity of both worker and family' (Seabury, 1985, p. 356). The emphasis on early decision-making in permanency planning can lead to burdening parents with unrealistic demands and expectations. The parents' failure to meet expectations is sometimes used as a reason for requesting termination of parental rights in court. Workers should be aware of this danger. They can use the process of negotiating an agreement as a way of clarifying and testing with the family what is realistic, and also determining what the agency must contribute to attain the agreed-upon goals.

Flexibility The agreement should not be cast in stone; it should be used flexibly as a tool rather than as an end in itself. It is open to change through discussion between family members and workers. 'Unlike a legal contract which is strictly binding once parties sign, a social work contract is more tentative and represents a dynamic, flexible plan rather than a set of strict rules' (Seabury, 1985 p. 355). It should 'be distinguished from court-ordered actions, which can only be changed by the court' (Seabury, 1985, p. 356).

To guard against rigidity, the agreement should include 'provisions for reformulation or renegotiation by mutual consent as circumstances change, problems are resolved, or the focus of intervention alters' (Maluccio and Marlow, 1974, p. 34). However, the emphasis on flexibility should not be taken to mean that the agreement has no force or that it should not be taken seriously. On the contrary, all parties should understand that it is an important document; that it should be considered carefully and thoughtfully; and that it can be changed only for valid reasons. It is also useful and appropriate to specify the consequences or sanctions that may ensue if any party does not follow through with the agreement.

Responsiveness To be used as a flexible tool, the agreement needs to be responsive or adapted to the particular qualities, styles, and needs of each client. For this reason, there should be careful assessment of clients within their significant environment.

The agreement is not developed in a vacuum, and it is not a routine or mechanistic event. It is a unique document which is based on comprehensive understanding of a client's situation, needs, and qualities, including their ethnic and racial characteristics. As it evolves on the basis of careful assessment of clients and their needs, the agreement can serve as a guide to treatment or service delivery.

Limitations The agreement is not a panacea. As with any tool or concept, it requires considerable skill and knowledge. It also has limitations and can be abused, as a result of such aspects as the inequality of power between parents and practitioners; the danger of using it to oppress or burden parents and families; and the difficulty of achieving mutuality between clients and social workers (Maluccio, 1979; Mayer and Timms, 1970; Rojeck and Collins, 1987; Seabury, 1979).

The contract or agreement has in fact been portrayed as a tool appropriate mainly for work with white, middle-class clients, or as a 'con-trick' that can further oppress clients, especially those from poor or minority groups (Rojek and Collins, 1987). It is therefore important to be alert to potential abuses and limitations in use of the agreement. Social workers need to build in safeguards and use approaches that enhance each family member's capacity for engaging in the process. This is

107

especially crucial in situations involving clients such as children and youth, persons with limited education or intellectual capacity, and those speaking another language. Similarly, client-worker differences in race, ethnicity, culture, socio-economic status, education, age, etc. need to be taken into account.

Principles and techniques for maximizing the use of the agreement and limiting its potential abuses have been delineated elsewhere (Corden and Preston-Shoot, 1987; Maluccio, Fein and Olmstead, 1986; Seabury, 1979 and 1985). As these authors show, ways can be found to involve most clients in the process, as long as workers are guided by values such as respect for the client's right to self-determination.

AGREEMENTS IN FOSTER FAMILY CARE OF ADOLESCENTS

How can agreements, particularly those that are written, be used in foster family care of adolescents? This section considers this question, covering these aspects:

- making placement decisions;
- principles in using agreements; and
- advantages and disadvantages of using agreements.

Making placement decisions

While the procedures by which agreements are formulated vary, all have in common a desire to make decisions regarding the objectives of a placement and the roles and tasks of the various participants. A great deal of preliminary negotiation and discussion invariably precedes any agreement meeting and there is thus a sense in which the making of an agreement is the fulfilment of a number of processes that have together contributed to the placement. Social workers will have initiated the search for a family placement, usually as a result of a decision at a case conference or team meeting. This decision will itself have been reached as a consequence of an assessment of the young person's needs and a preliminary formulation of the objectives of the intended fostering placement.

Efforts by specialist workers will then have led to the matching of the adolescent and his or her needs with a particular foster family. Extensive work should have been carried out by social workers and, in some cases, residential workers to prepare the young person for family placement. This preparation should again have helped to clarify what the objectives and expectations of the young person are, while clearing out of the way the numerous mis-expectations that invariably abound.

While individual circumstances vary, it is apparent that any decision to place a young person in a foster family involves a series of highly significant preparatory exercises that are crucial to the formulation of more detailed plans for the placement. Agreements are not intended to be a substitute for these activities; what they ideally do is bring this work to a point of fruition, by sharing prior discussions with all the participants in a placement, and by clarifying and making explicit areas of agreement and disagreement. An agreement meeting has no special magic, although it can have powerful symbolic importance and the bringing together of the different parties can effect change and redirection priorities. Perhaps most importantly, it produces a written record of decisions, aims and tasks that can be referred back to by all participants, and that can be the basis for future evaluation of the success of the placement as a whole, and of its specified aims.

When the birth family remain involved, further discussions will have to be sought to clarify with them the purpose of the placement, their role in relation to it, and their continuing relationship with the young person.

Principles in using agreements

There has now been considerable experience of the use of placement agreements in specialist adolescent fostering programs in the UK. Such programs are characterized by an emphasis upon time-limited, task-focused work with often difficult adolescents and customarily provide more substantial remuneration to the foster parents, who participate fully in the formulation of the placement objectives. This section will seek to outline some of the practice implications of the use of agreements that have been developed from the experience of operating one such small scale program in the UK.

As discussed earlier in this chapter, clarity is essential in the use of agreements in social work practice. Clarity, however, must be based upon the attainable, especially in foster family care. There is no purpose in having an agreement around an aim that cannot be achieved. Goals must therefore be reasonable and expectations well judged. Objectives and tasks must be specific if the goal of clarity is to have meaning. The agreement must be written in language that everybody sharing in it understands. Efforts must be made to ensure that this is the case. Silence should never be assumed to mean comprehension, particularly since both parents and adolescents may be fearful or hesitant to share their views or question the worker's thinking and recommendations.

Confusion often arises about the different roles and responsibilities of social workers in relation to a placement. At its simplest, this can mean that the foster parents and adolescents may be unsure as to whom to turn for support and guidance.

Therefore it is essential that the discrete responsibilities of the various social workers involved are clarified. Communication channels need to be made explicit so that all parties are seen to share the same expectations. At its simplest this means that all participants need to know what to tell to whom.

While most placements will have as their eventual aim the preparation of the young person for independence, it must be recognized that this process is made up of a large number of transitional tasks. An agreement needs to place these sometimes minor developments in sharp forms so that achievements can be recognized. All placements have problems and if these are allowed to dominate the consciousness of the participants an overly negative attitude can result. Positive developments should be held on to and highlighted, as the fulfilment of a relatively minor objective can at least show that all is not bleak.

The production of an agreement, even where it records areas of disagreement, should be based upon open participation and the sharing of information and can thus contribute to developing the idea of the placement as an effort in teamwork. All parties are seen to have jobs and work to carry out, although clearly the young person and the foster family have the most to wrestle with. What is emphasized, however, is that achieving the goal of the placement is a task shared between the foster family, the young person and his or her family and the professionals involved. This emphasis is reinforced by introducing from the outset an idea of the ending of the placement. The question of how long it will last is always asked and an answer, however imprecise, always expected and given. This sense of the finite, of a time limit, is perhaps a special benefit for teenagers whose lives are naturally moving towards change and the goals of independence.

Agreements provide a record of decisions at a particular point. Mutual agreements address themselves to the overall purpose of the placement but also set a series of tasks to be attempted and completed. All agreements must therefore concern themselves with the process of review and evaluation. As suggested earlier, if an agreement is to have life as a usable tool, it must not be seen to acquire the status of 'a tablet of stone'. A time and date for review must be explicitly stated, as must the means by which a meeting may be called in an emergency to discuss changes and renegotiations that may need to be made.

All participants must feel that they have the right to call a meeting that will be held as a matter of urgency. Agreements will usually state that termination of the placement should not occur until such a meeting has taken place, and that 28 days notice should be given by either the young person or the foster parent.

It is perhaps unnecessary to restate that an agreement cannot be a binding contract. Yet, there is a danger that it can be seen to give a somewhat unrealistic quasi-legal quality to a process that is, of necessity, circumscribed by a whole range of contingencies. An important point is that the agreement provides a basis for planned termination, rather than the all too common experience of removal at a point of crisis. The idea of giving notice does, however, bring to the forefront the principle that the agreement is based upon duties and responsibilities and that it makes explicit the participation of all parties.

Advantages and disadvantages of using agreements

A group of experienced foster parents in one adolescent fostering program, who meet weekly with their social worker, was asked to comment on what it saw as the advantages and disadvantages of written placement agreements.

Advantages Among the positive qualities they listed were:

1 The process of sitting down to make the agreement has value in itself, as it brings together everybody involved in the placement and physically demonstrates the team approach.
2 It helps in setting goals.
3 It makes the young person part of the decision-making process and can act as a control on his/her behavior.
4 It helps avoid confusion.
5 It offers boundaries and security.
6 It acts as a baseline for development.
7 It helps the young person look towards the time when he/she will be living independently.
8 It forces everybody to think of what should happen after the placement ends.

Disadvantages Agreements do not in themselves make successful placement nor does the formulation of a written agreement ensure that the parties involved continue to follow its decisions. There are dangers that, unless birth parents, foster parents and adolescents believe in the value of written agreements, they will come to see them as bureaucratic hurdles that have to be overcome before the placement can begin.

In the same group of experienced foster parents of adolescents, it was clear that a few of them had experienced agreements as generally helpful; others had seen them as a useful starting point but of little relevance once the young person was living with them.

Among the disadvantages noted by these foster parents were that the agreement:

1 Can be disregarded;
2 Can be too idealistic;
3 Can be too static;
4 Can be too rigid;
5 Can be used as a weapon;
6 Can be very time consuming;
7 Can pretend that the young people are parties to the decisions when they are effectively powerless.

In addition, foster parents consistently reported that the agreements failed to deal with most of the issues that troubled them in their day-to-day life with the teenagers. Instead, they saw them more as a formal review of certain troublesome issues such as careers and schooling. The message that came across strongly was that they failed to address the everyday questions of discipline that cumulatively can lead to a crisis over relatively minor issues.

Circumstances in which agreements can be used positively

The small consumer survey of specialist foster parents outlined above was useful in providing information from foster parents themselves about the most helpful use of agreements: to address specific tangible problems. The foster parents thought that agreements could be best used in providing more guidance on the formulation of what might be called 'family rules'. This would involve the elucidation not only of expectations of behavior but also the development of clearly defined sanctions for the violation of these family norms. More positively, rewards could be agreed for compliance either with these rules as a whole, or with specific behavioral expectations. Thomas (1988), a fostering officer in a social services department, endorses this view, emphasizing that the promotion of competence is a major goal in the making of written agreements (see also Maluccio, 1981).

Furthermore, the use of agreements has to recognize the unequal power relationship between social workers and foster parents. Thomas (1988) believes that this may inhibit honesty in foster parents who are fearful of challenging social workers in case the placement is terminated. Conversely, a foster parent in an informal survey carried out by Simm in his agency said that she did not like to contact the young person's social worker about problems he was exhibiting because she always felt that the social worker was frightened that the foster parent was threatening to terminate the placement. What this foster parent desired, therefore, was an agreement that spelt out other actions that could and should be done before reaching that ultimate point of crisis. If an agreement does not concern itself directly with such issues, then it is in danger of concentrating too much on the goals and neglecting the beginning of the long process of achieving a successful placement and effective preparation for interdependent living.

From his experience, Thomas (1988) has identified issues and topics, many of which relate to daily family life, that lend themselves to the use of agreements in foster care for adolescents. These include the following:

– Are there specific things that the young person needs to learn (for example, to talk about defined problems, to manage anger, to acquire tangible life skills)?

– Are there activities that are of particular importance to a youngster? Can the agreement specify a commitment to these continuing? What are the practical arrangements?

– School – which one, what transport is needed?

– Money – how much pocket money? How will clothing be purchased?

– Wages – how much will be handed over to foster parents?

– Household chores – what is the young person expected to do?

– Care of pets – who is responsible – who pays for food?

– Social life – clear rules about informing the family about coming home times and whereabouts; owning a front door key.

– Activities, for example, homework or sport – what is to be the involvement and commitment from foster parents?

- Sharing bedrooms – who will be responsible for what?

- Details about handling other equally important issues, including substance abuse, stealing, swearing, eating problems.

- Preparation for self-sufficiency, for example, who is responsible for getting the young person housing and how will this be done?

(Thomas, 1988)

Practice applications

Translating the ideas about using agreements into practice sometimes appears a daunting task. During the last year, in the UK, the National Foster Care Association has been piloting a pro forma for an initial placement agreement in several social services departments. At the time of writing, a working party is evaluating the results of this experiment but a specialist fostering officer in one of the local authorities which participated has published elsewhere the evaluation made in his agency (Thomas, 1988). Thomas found that, although there was initial resistance to using agreements, on the grounds that they would create more work, the favourable outcome, in terms of satisfied participants, more than justified the means. He concluded that agreements provide a clear framework for intervention but, as suggested earlier in this chapter, they can only be a part of good practice and are not a replacement for the personal contacts between workers, young people, birth families and foster families that achieve progress in a placement. It is with these thoughts in mind that, with their kind permission, there follows National Foster Care Association's draft Initial Placement Agreement form and a case example of how it has been in practice in the piloting stage of development. At the time of writing, the working party is still modifying the form. The final version may differ in some minor respects from the one presented here. Readers might like to contact National Foster Care Association for further details.

INITIAL PLACEMENT AGREEMENT

Notes

1 Whenever possible natural parents will need to be participants to this agreement. Apart from them, the child, and the foster parents, there should be a minimum number of people

1 *Participants to agreement*

participating – only those actively involved in the carrying out of the agreement.

2 *What problems led to the placement being necessary and the child not being able to live at home?*	2 *Problem* i.e. what is now wrong

These should be specific and identify conditions and/or behaviors – these should be additional to a careful note of any allegations upheld in court (if applicable) or presented as reasons for care (if applicable). WRITE THE PROBLEMS IN SIMPLE CLEAR TERMS. Note if different participants have different opinions.

3 *What goal(s) will everyone work towards?* The goal(s) must be one(s) that can EASILY BE ACHIEVED. Keep them simple and clear, and list in order of priority.	3 *Goal* i.e. what is needed
4 *Will any existing house rules conflict with the goal(s)?*	4 *House rules* for the placement

When will the detailed house rules be discussed and agreed?
House rules (e.g. times to be in by, arrangements for visitors) only need discussion here if they are likely to conflict with the goal(s) noted in (3)

5 *How long is the placement to last? When is/are the goal(s) above to be achieved?*	5 *Time limit*
6 *Brief details of who, what, when and why are needed here.*	6 *Tasks* i.e. who will do what to achieve the goal(s)?

Check to see if there is a necessary *order* for doing the tasks, and check to see that no one thinks there are particular *obstacles* in the way of completing them. As before try and keep them simple and clear.

a) for agency and social worker
b) for foster parents
c) for child

	and own parents d) for others
7 *Who will visit who, when and why? (e.g. statutory visits, contact worker visits to foster parents etc.)*	7 *Frequency and purpose of social work contact*
8 *Full details of contact (who, when, where, how, and why), and of the help to be given.*	8 *Contact with natural family*
9 *When will progress towards the goal be reviewed?* Will there be a number of reviews before the time limit noted in (5)?	9 *Review of progress.*
10 *What are the plans for the child if the goal(s) is/are not achievable?* Give a broad indication of the plans.	10 *Contingency plans*
11 *What are the means of dealing with any participant's dissatisfactions, or for changing this agreement?* Note the name(s) of the social worker(s) who will arrange any necessary meetings to discuss dissatisfaction or changes.	11 *Dissatisfactions and changes*

Prime responsibility for work with the natural family during this placement will rest with

Signatures

There follows an example of how this proforma for an agreement has been used in practice.

INITIAL PLACEMENT AGREEMENT

1 *Participants to the agreement*

Tracy Baker	Young person
Mrs Iris Baker	Birth mother
John and Sarah Livingstone	Foster parents
Brian Simpson	Tracy's social worker

| Jennifer Hall | Social worker to Special Foster Care Scheme |
| Barry Robinson | Social worker with Intermediate Treatment Team |

2 *What problems led to the placement being necessary and the young person not being able to live at home?*
  i Mrs Baker's drinking problem which led to
    – a lack of consistency
    – the children not going to school regularly
    – unpredictable behavior towards Tracy
  ii Mrs Baker not consistently wanting Tracy at home
  iii Tracy's unhappiness in the family led to her asking to come into care
  iv Tracy was beyond parental control

3 *What goal(s) will everyone work towards?*
  i *School*: Tracy to complete her schooling at Worthinton School until the end of the next school year – July 1988 (in first instance);
  ii *Living in the foster family*: The Livingstones to provide Tracy with security so that Tracy can make a realistic decision about the future – whether she wants to move on to eventual self-sufficiency or return to her family;
  iii *Maintaining links with the birth family*: Tracy needs opportunities to assess the realism of a return home – both for her and for her mother. This can be done by planned visits home;
  iv *Sport and leisure*: Tracy needs support and encouragement in following her sporting and leisure activities;
  v *Managing behaviour*: Tracy needs to learn how to handle not getting her own way all the time. Tracy agrees with this.

4 *House rules*
House rules to be negotiated with John and Sarah (see Tasks ii).

5 *How long is the placement to last?*
Until Tracy is 16, in the first instance; then, planning for leaving care at 18. This last two years could mean increased contact with Tracy's family (possible shared care) or the continuation of this placement or another one.

117

6 *Tasks: i.e. Who will do what to achieve the goals (listed in 3)?*

 i *School*

  a Livingstones to be responsible for Tracy's school attendance, to provide general support and encouragement with homework and to attend parents' evenings;

  b Livingstones to take Tracy to school;

  c Brian Simpson to sort out with the Education Department payment to foster family for mileage to and from school;

  d Tracy to go to school; also to put an effort into her work if she wants to do well, as she says she does.

 ii *Living in the foster family*

  a Livingstones to parent Tracy in the normal family/teenager model appropriate to Tracy's age;

  b Livingstones to be open and honest about their rules and expectations and to let social worker know about any rules under threat;

  c Tracy to agree in principle to abide by rules.

 iii *Maintaining links with the birth family*

  a Social worker to respond to Tracy's wish to see her family and make a definite visiting programme (details to be agreed in sub-agreement between all concerned);

  b Social worker to be in touch with Mrs Baker and, with her permission, Redborough Social Services Department, to assess home situation and ascertain her point of view on Tracy's welfare and access visits;

  c John, foster father, to take Tracy to visit her mother at pre-arranged times;

  d Tracy to be open and honest about communication she is having with her mother and her family;

  e Tracy to try to be honest with the foster parents and her social worker about what happens when she visits home and what the situation is really like for her;

  f Social worker, Brian Simpson, to plan to be, and make himself available to discuss this with Tracy;

  g Foster parents to note Tracy's behaviour before and after visits and to let social worker know.

   iv *Sport and leisure activities*
- a Barry Robinson, (Intermediate Treatment worker), to discuss programme of activities that his project can provide;
- b Tracy to co-operate with this.

   v *Tracy's behaviour*
Social worker, foster parents and Tracy to work on a programme of helping Tracy overcome her frustration when she does not get her own way.

6 *Frequency and purpose of social work contact*
   i *Brian Simpson*
- a Brian to see Tracy every 2–3 weeks at a minumum and as soon as possible after every visit home to help build positive communication between Tracy and her mother, Tracy and her foster parents and between Tracy's mother and the foster parents;
- b Brian to work directly with Mrs Baker on her relationship with Tracy;
- c Brian also to arrange statutory reviews.

   ii *Jennifer Hall*
- a Jennifer Hall to run weekly support meetings for all foster parents in the special adolescent project to provide them with opportunities for learning and development of skills;
- b John and Sarah Livingstone to attend these meetings.

   iii *Barry Robinson*
Barry Robinson to provide agreed Intermediate Treatment activities.

7 *Contact with the birth family*
   i Visits by Tracy to her mother's home to be agreed and arranged through Brian Simpson – written agreement to be developed about the visiting before first visit;
   ii Brian Simpson to accompany Tracy to her mother's home.

8 *Review of progress within 3 months*
   i Management of the house rules of the foster family to be reviewed at the end of 3 months;

   ii Tracy's visits home to be reviewed after each contact (but with the aim of establishing a regular pattern);

iii Earlier review can be requested by any signatory to the agreement.

9 *Review of goal achievement*
Goals to be reassessed at school-leaving age (but may be reviewed at any time at the request of any signatory).

10 *Contingency plans*
If placement ends unexpectedly or the goals prove unattainable, Talltrees reception children's home will provide emergency accommodation to allow for alternative plans to be made.

11 *Means of dealing with dissatisfactions or for changing the agreement*
Any participant can ask for a meeting to be called to discuss these issues. Jennifer Hall will arrange the meeting.

Prime responsibility for work with the birth family will rest with *Brian Simpson*.

Signatures

CONCLUSION

The experience of specialist adolescent fostering schemes in the UK suggests that very difficult young people can make considerable gains in foster family placements with explicitly stated and limited goals. It is of interest, for example, that of 42 placements enacted since 1977 in Oxfordshire, only 3 have disrupted. This rate reflects the findings of Berridge and Cleaver (1987) that specialist fostering tends to be less vulnerable to disruption. It is also considerably lower than rates reported in research on traditional foster home breakdown in the UK and the US (Aldgate and Hawley, 1986; Berridge and Cleaver, 1987; and Block and Libowitz, 1983).

While the placement agreement is only part of a process, and as has been suggested above inevitably throws up its own problems, it can be seen to have a role in defining goals, laying stress on openness and, perhaps most importantly, helping the foster parents to feel valued and listened to. It also goes some way to making the young person an author in his/her own life rather than, as has so often been stressed by 'graduates' from care, a powerless object upon whom decisions are imposed.

Agreements can then be seen to have a number of benefits but they are not a panacea for all problems. An agreement is essentially worthwhile to the extent that all participants, and particularly the young person and the foster family, believe in its value, and to the degree to which it provides a usable, flexible and dynamic framework for the infinitely complex set of contingencies facing the placement. It cannot hope to address itself to all problems that arise. What it should seek to do is provide a system within which such problems can be dealt with at an early stage.

8 Programs for interdependent living
Richard P. Barth

The benefits of recent permanency planning statutes in the United States are significant but may contribute to the welfare of adolescents least of all. As noted in Chapter 1, more than one-quarter of the children in foster care in the United States enter care as adolescents (Hornby and Collins, 1981; Timberlake and Verdieck, 1987). Placement prevention is particularly difficult among adolescents who, more than younger children, enter foster care because of their behavior problems rather than, or in addition to, inadequacies in the home. In addition, few adolescents return to their birth families, and fewer still are adopted (Hornby and Collins, 1981). As a result, in both the US and UK, there is growing concern with programs to prepare adolescents for 'emancipation' from care (Stone, 1987; Stein and Carey, 1986; Barth, 1986). This chapter reviews some of those programs following a summary of selected findings from studies of young people who have left care.

RESEARCH ON LEAVING CARE

Studies of children who have grown up in foster care are scarce. Moreover, as suggested in Chapter 4, most studies do not distinguish between individuals who had significant stays in foster care but left before the age of majority, those who entered foster care as adolescents and were discharged at the age of majority, and those who grew up in foster care and left at the age of majority. Available studies also assess outcomes with different measures and measure different contributors to outcome.

Studies on outcomes for former foster children show that many entered care because of behavioral or personal handicaps, as well as family-related problems. With abridged educations, no borrowing power, and scanty guidance or encouragement, these youths are expected to negotiate successfully the vagaries of a society requiring more and more preparation for first jobs and capital for obtaining an education and a residence. Yet reviews of outcomes for foster children in the US and the UK also suggest that some have the capacity to adjust rather well (Barth, 1986; Maluccio and Fein, 1985; Triseliotis, 1980). This capacity differs, of course, depending on their experiences prior to discharge from care.

As indicated in Chapter 4, what has emerged from both the consumer surveys of young people who have left care and the studies recounting the views of their foster parents and social workers is the inadequacy of preparation for transition into adulthood (see Porter, 1983; Stein and Carey, 1986; and Chapter 5 of this book). Some researchers have found that workers and caregivers underscore the importance of providing help to young people with concrete needs and tangible skills in such areas as money management (Chestnut, 1985). Yet others note that service providers over-emphasize the importance of tangible services, and should, instead, first and foremost endeavor to enhance the adolescent's self-image and interpersonal skills (Beyer, 1986). Increasingly, researchers point to the need of adolescents in care for help in both tangible and intangible areas (Porter, 1983; Stone, 1987; and Chapters 4 and 5 in this book).

Much more needs to be learned about adolescents leaving foster care in order to contribute to the development and operation of programs preparing youngsters for self-sufficiency. In particular, information is required regarding age, gender, race and ethnicity, educational achievements, health, and mental health of youth moving toward discharge from care; experience with prior foster, adoption, or guardianship arrangements; and relationships with birth parents. In addition, knowledge is needed about the extent to which new materials on preparing adolescents for interdependent living are used and their influence on the performance of foster parents. We also need information about the effectiveness of methods used to teach required skills; and the support that should be provided when adolescents attempt to use those skills to meet new challenges in their post-discharge environments.

PROGRAMS FOR SELF-SUFFICIENCY

Although much remains to be learned, a variety of approaches to preparation of youth for self-sufficiency have emerged in the field of child welfare. These are relatively new and, unlike programs in mental health and developmental disabilities, few pre-date the 1970s. Programs that have developed to supplement the emancipation efforts of traditional foster family care vary along a dimension of options. These include:

– standard foster family care;
– specialist foster family care with the specific aim of preparing youths for full independence;
– supervised lodgings;
– group homes;
– supervised apartments; and
– 'independent living' subsidy programs;

Standard foster family care

Whereas foster parent training in general is increasingly becoming more commonplace in child welfare both in the US and the UK, no state or county, to this author's knowledge in the US, includes more than the minimum of training and promoting preparation for emancipation from care in their initial foster parent training programs. If long-term foster family care is to be a viable option, as suggested in Chapters 1 and 5, then it will be increasingly necessary for foster parents to receive training at various strategic points throughout the placement so that they may meet the developmental needs of their foster adolescents. As Clarkson and Whistlecraft suggest 'Whilst an initial program provides an information and skills base, there appears to be a need to offer additional and more specialist training to foster parents at particular stages, for example on behavior management of young children, adolescents' behavior, preparation for independence, sexuality and so-on'. From their practice experience in one UK social services department, the authors recommend the development of training modules that build upon the initial programs to 'follow foster parents as they move through and develop their fostering career' (Clarkson and Whistlecraft, 1987, p. 35).

Specialist foster care

Specialist foster placements offer additional hope for success both in the US and the UK, in preparing young people for emancipation from care. An important UK program, which has been widely replicated in other parts of the country, was that developed in Kent in the early 1980s which used foster care as a 'bridge' between residential group care and independent living for young people emancipating from care (see Hazel, 1981). Swedish thinking provided four guiding principles for the project:

> *normalization*, that a child then living away from his own family should have as normal a life as possible; *localization*, the child's right to remain in his local community; *voluntariness*, that as far as possible the child and his family should be in agreement with decisions made; and right to *participation*, again by child and family in all decisions affecting them. (Shaw and Hipgrave, 1983, p. 27)

The success of the Kent scheme was due to careful planning and evaluation, along with an emphasis on families retaining links with their foster youngsters after official emancipation from care. By contrast, some other projects have been so rigidly defined by time limits that youngsters have found themselves in lonely apartments or bed-sits almost on the very day of their 18th birthday, an outcome that can hardly be described as desirable. A recent exception is 'Compass', a project developed jointly by Barnardo's and Surrey Social Services Department, which is rooted in an ecological approach, developing family placements for 13–17-year-olds who would otherwise remain in unsuitable residential homes or temporary foster family care. Compass does not aim to substitute for a permanent family. Compass families are encouraged to build up links with birth families and to help young people develop a network of local contacts and interests (Barnardo's, 1988).

Shaw and Hipgrave (1983) provide a comprehensive survey of 'specialist' foster care in the UK, of which adolescent projects comprise only a part. They suggest that many UK schemes have been inspired by similar projects in North America (Jones, 1978; Tozer, 1979). To complement Shaw and Hipgrave's (1983) work, the development of specialist foster care in the US has been usefully reviewed by Bryant (1981).Since his review, as noted in Chapter 10, agencies are beginning to consider the use of specialist training for foster parents that is focused on preparation of young people for interdependent living and self-sufficiency. To this end, training materials are increasingly available (see Chapter 10 and also Mauzerall, 1983; Dvorak and Mason, 1985; Guerney, 1978).

Supervised lodgings

A current difficulty with foster family care, as suggested in Chapters 4 and 5, is that it ends officially when a youth reaches the age of majority.

The need for interdependent living still remains. In the UK, there has been some attempt to offer one alternative by using supervised lodgings but this facility has not been without its problems. Families have sometimes found themselves acting as full foster families to youngsters who are unemployed and have many other personal problems, but without the normal advantage of agency support. A recent scheme in Kent, Rented Accommodation for Teenagers (RAFT), is an innovative project that asks families to provide a base for young people who have left care and are homeless. It is connected to a youth center that offers day and evening support, counseling and activities for young people and monthly support groups for their RAFT families. The knowledge that the young people will be constructively occupied during the day has encouraged families to join the project as they feel a sense of shared responsibility for the young person's welfare. Additionally, the staff at the center have co-operated with the RAFT social workers (Hazel, 1988).

Group homes

One option to prepare young people for emancipation from care has been to use group homes for the transitional period between foster family care and complete independence from the agency and care. Some agencies have developed new group homes or transformed established group homes as specialized homes for 'independent living' preparation. The central idea is to offer an interdependent situation that fosters assessment and learning of needed skills.

An example is the Casey Family Program's Independent Living Project (Mauzerall, 1983), in which group homes are reserved for emancipating minors and staff are trained to assist their efforts. Youths stay about six months and the program stresses the use of contracts between youth and group home parents as an essential part of their services, reflecting the principles delineated in Chapter 7. Other than the structure of these contracts, residents are unbridled by the typical rules of foster care. Their support checks are distributed directly to them and they pay 'rent' to their foster parents/landlords. Limited evaluations by project staff indicate that initial results are promising. There are similar newly developed projects in the UK, for example, in Nottingham (Woodward, 1986), Bolton and Cheshire (details from National Foster Care Association).

Supervised apartments

Supervised apartments give youth still more freedom and responsibility. There are three examples included here, two from the US and one from the UK. Drawing on a model of supervised living arrangements common to services for mental or physical disabilities, the first example is the Hope Center for Youth in Texas, which has developed a Supervised Apartment Living Program for soon-to-be-discharged minors (Furrh, 1983). Adolescents who are at least 16 years old live in one of two apartment complexes – segregated by gender. These complexes are licensed as half-way houses and each has 20 residents and a ratio of one staff for five youths. Skills training for self-sufficiency is comprehensive, covering such topics as financial responsibility, vocational skills, job finding, consumer skills, use of community resources, and interpersonal skills. Although young people from juvenile justice, mental health, and mental retardation are also served, this living arrangement is a prototype for other child welfare programs. This particular program seems to have found the right recipe for success. The staff's follow-up evaluation concluded that more than 70 per cent of participants moved successfully into independent living, with 20 per cent returning home and only 10 per cent returning to the care of another agency or becoming not traceable.

A second program, which has met with mixed success, has been Crossroads, a supervised apartment program for young people who are preparing to live on their own. The evaluation of this program clarifies the dimensions of supervised apartment programs (Wimpfheimer, 1986), pointing to its strengths and weaknesses. Residence at Crossroads comes complete with life classes and group counseling. Youth with serious substance abuse problems, emotional disturbance, or criminal behavior are not accepted into the program. A strength is that the program includes youths from group or foster care, as well as others who had been living at home or with friends or in sub-standard housing such as garages or motels. An example of a typical client could be an 18-year-old living in a chaotic situation with perhaps, some emotional and substance abuse problems, a history of delinquency, and a poor school record.

A major problem has been that young people often do not use the program as planned. In Crossroads, young people were at first expected to complete all independent living and socialization modules prior to discharge, but this standard was lifted after the staff realized that young people were leaving whenever they felt ready. The anticipated length of stay was also different in practice than in planning – the six to eight months' expected stay was too long for many young people who refused to enter the program or left early; many stayed less than two months. In the evaluation of this program, youth were most critical about the rules and the curfew and most positive about learning specific life skills like banking, cooking, and job search.

Despite the apparent need, the recruitment and retention of residents for such programs is difficult for several reasons. Supervised apartment programs that require young people to be current residents of foster or group care and exclude young people living without adequate housing, will find it difficult to keep their programs full. Secondly, young people in foster and group homes are often uninterested in moving to another residence simply because it permits and promotes more self-sufficiency. They may experience supervised living arrangements as embarrassing. Indeed, post-discharge interviews with Crossroads clients indicated that they often lied to employers about their home address and interpreted living in a supervised setting as a symbol of personal failure. It is therefore not surprising that many young people develop what they believe to be more suitable arrangements with their former foster families (Wimpfheimer, 1986).

A third program, in the UK, has attempted to resolve some of the problems of Crossroads by offering hostel accommodation in half-way houses that can then be exchanged for permanent tenancies with a housing association. This program, 209 Iffley Road (Cherwell Housing), has been established in Oxford since 1984. Young people leaving care who opt for and are chosen for the program, go to a hostel managed by a housing association, from which, if the placement works out satisfactorily, they can move to a permanent tenancy of an apartment (flat) managed by the same association. The program has been successful, mainly because the youth are well motivated, knowing that they will be de-stigmatized by ultimately becoming submerged in the general apartment-renting population. Further expansion is planned in the development of supported interdependent accommodation at the first stage, by introducing bed-sitting rooms and small apartments as an alternative to the hostel. These will be characterized by the provision of out-reach workers, based in the hostel, who will help the young people through the difficult transition from an environment with staff *in situ*, to life on their own in the community.

Interdependent living subsidy programs

Another innovation involves subsidizing private-sector housing for youth. The Oregon Children's Division Services' Independent Living

Subsidy Program (ILSP) typifies such programs and pr
adolescents with start-up apartment costs and stipends for contɪ
living in residences of their choice (Halm, 1980). Living arrangem
are negotiated by youth with landlords. Social workers meet with youth
twice monthly. Some social workers see this as a strength of the program,
while others view it as an expensive and burdensome requirement
(Altorfer and O'Donnell, 1978). The average length of stay is just short
of one and one-half years (Halm, 1980).

A Canadian program in Montreal, Youth Horizons, is a cross between
a supervised apartment program and a subsidy program. Service
agreements are signed between social service agencies and landlords who
agree to provide housing and minimal supervision. Apartment buildings
are rarely used because landlords and/or managers are not interested in
the extra problems. More commonly, clients live in duplexes or private
homes with self-contained units. The agency agrees to monitor clients
and be responsible for rent and behavior problems, moving the client
elsewhere if necessary. The model has been found to be least effective
with the youngest clients, because the transition from their previous
living situations to this program was too drastic. A more intermediate
setting and/or more preparation before placement in independent living
seemed necessary. Many of the youths were not interested in social work
services and were resistant to demand made by the program staff in such
areas as employment, school, and life skills. The program no longer
serves young adults exiting the child welfare system, and has changed its
focus to young adults in the mental health system. The shift has occurred
as a result of a lack of referrals from child welfare agencies and lack of
appeal to youth who had other alternatives.

Some similar programs of both supervised and interdependent living
subsidy programs have been developed in the UK, pioneered by the
investigative work of Shelter (the National Campaign for the Homeless)
and First Key, under its former name of Home Base. This is a resource
and advisory agency seeking to improve the life chances of young people
who have been in local authority care. Robson (1987) reports that in the
early 1980s there was considerable initiative from central government to
provide capital funding for housing projects, the aim of which was 'to
develop intermediate, supportive accommodation' to aid the transition
between a foster home or children's home and a sparse apartment or
bedsit. Many of the projects over the last few years have been developed
through a partnership between housing associations and local voluntary
social work agencies and, less frequently, statutory social services.

Robson argues that these projects need to become part of a whole range of provision rather than be seen as a single 'one off' solution to the problems of young people leaving care. A range of provisions is necessary for two reasons:

First there is a wide variety of issues and stages which young people leaving care face. Second, young people in care and leaving care are not a group with a single identity. As a result, they have a number of different needs requiring response. Issues to be faced will consist of a combination of the following: housing; coping with practicalities of independent living; building support networks; employment, education and training; access to health care and welfare benefits and rights, together with the broader issue of money and poverty; and for many, social discrimination and institutional racism. (Robson, 1987, pp. 20–21)

PROGRAMS DEALING WITH THE ACQUISITION OF OTHER SKILLS

Parallel to the needs outlined by Robson, several program models have been developed in the US to assist young people in the transition to adulthood. They include:

– education and scholarship programs;
– pre- and post-emancipation groups and services;
– self-help groups;
– mentor, befriending programs;
– employment services;
– intensive case co-ordination.

Education and scholarship programs

Follow-up studies have identified the exceptional educational needs of foster children (Festinger, 1983; Triseliotis, 1980; Jackson, 1988). Limited finances and educational preparation make the likelihood of attending college after foster care doubtful. The failure to attend college not only limits a foster child's future income, but often ends their immediate post-high school support. In some states in the US, foster care grants can be extended until age 21 to allow young people to continue their education. (In the UK, there is no parallel provision but local authorities can provide money directly for young people to continue their education up to the age of 21.) In the states in the US which offer this opportunity, pursuing higher education provides the additional advantage of continuity of care during young people's struggles to remediate their educational disadvantages. Unfortunately, at least five states have laws prohibiting all foster care payments beyond age 18. This also reflects the current situation with regard to foster care placements in the UK, although occasionally loopholes in the law allow young people to remain with their foster families until age 19.

The Foster Care League, a non-profit-making private agency in the US, attempts to help foster children achieve adequate educational preparation for college (Dolan and O'Neill, 1983). This agency serves as a liaison between social service agencies and private boarding schools in New England, to arrange placements and scholarships for foster children. Some 65 private schools have granted scholarships of 50 per cent or more of the costs. Agencies pay the standard or special foster care rates. Foster children maintain contact with their foster families and return home during vacations, and foster parents are reimbursed at a daily rate. Five states are now using the Foster Care League's no-fee placement service. The program warrants evaluation .

Additional education services are essential for foster children. For example, the Foster Youth Services Program in California provides auxiliary employment and educational counseling to foster children from kindergarten through their final grade (Seashore, 1986). Child welfare workers, foster parents, or classroom teachers inform this agency when a new foster child enrolls in school. After consultation with the child's birth and foster parents, the agency's staff contact the foster child, who may receive group or individual tutoring and employment counseling from the staff members as they visit various schools. As part of these contacts with staff members or in additional meetings, the youth may receive counseling to facilitate their accommodation to their new schools or other new settings. To improve the children's ability to adjust and achieve, the program staff also consult with classroom teachers.

Roughly one out of four children served by the Foster Youth Services program is in special education. Agency staff ensure that a young person's special education status is known to the school authorities, facilitate individualized planning, and track down required vaccination records so that the young person can gain speedy admission to the school. The staff also advocate with school districts that are reluctant to complete the required, and costly, individualized planning process for foster youths who may soon move away. The staff also screen for institutional abuse among educable and trainable mentally retarded youth who reside in foster or group homes. An evaluation of the effectiveness of the Foster Youth Services program documents gains in academic performance and behavior for participants (Seashore, 1986). As this project has shown, educational enrichment is an important adjunct to interdependent living services.

Pre- and post-emancipation groups and services

Services to prepare adolescents for self-sufficiency are largely restricted to specialized programs. Adolescents who do not participate in such programs – as is true for most – are not likely to find help with planning their impending emancipation or to find assistance during emancipation. Life Planning Services for Older Children, a project in Minnesota, is designed to help youth aged 10 to 16 who have been freed for adoption but whose family status and emancipation plans remain unclear (McDermott, 1987). This joint effort of voluntary and public child welfare agencies and the juvenile court supports outreach efforts to identify such youth, offers group and individual counseling to assist adolescents' efforts to consider their options, and helps develop plans for independent living. Prior to leaving care, social workers help youth identify relationships that approximate continuous family relationships or that show promise of developing into family-like relationships. They also encourage interested adults to maintain a relationship with the young people before and after discharge from care. Supportive services are provided to the adult and adolescent, to help them explore the implications of their commitment and planning for their future. From a survey of caseworkers' concerns, the authors also derived areas of consideration in developing life skills groups. Peer interrelations and self-esteem were seen as an area for concern for foster children. Social skills in relating to authority were also addressed. Sexuality was also a major concern and fittingly so, in view of high risk-taking behavior among teens that may lead to unwanted pregnancies and to sexually transmitted diseases.

Another example of pre-emancipation services is the Salvation Army's (1982) program which is designed to help teenagers take charge of their own lives through gaining information about themselves, their physical and emotional growth and development, and available community resources. The program uses a group work format, and emphasis is placed on selection of the group leader. Group leaders must be knowledgeable about adolescent development, group dynamics, and community resources, in addition to being committed to working with young people. Discussion topics include self-understanding, resource development, getting and keeping a job, citizenship, health (including substance abuse), intimate relationships, marriage and children.

This program is one of few with available evaluation data (Hofman and Cole, 1983). Youth reportedly 'gained in knowledge and self-confidence' by the end of the program. A later assessment of the continuing impact showed that two years after completing it, participants were still 'using the knowledge and insights gained'. More than 80 per cent were still at school. They were reportedly better able to recognize and handle peer pressure, stay in school or employment, and avoid unplanned pregnancies. Young people rated 'making personal decisions about my life' as the most important learning. The highest value was on 'getting along with parents or guardians' and on 'positive feelings about myself'. Robson (1987) argues for the development of similar groups in the UK.

Self-help groups

In an era in which self-help groups are increasing in number and acceptance by professionals and lay persons, foster-child self-help groups receive minimal attention. Adolescent self-help groups have traditionally had difficulty maintaining membership and momentum (Barth, 1983), although some notable exceptions like Ala-teen and Daughters and Sons United in the US, and the National Association of Young People in Care and Black and in Care in the UK, suggest the potential for such efforts. Success may well be linked to a recognition that, within the general group of young people leaving care, there are individuals with many differing needs. In the UK, for example, there has been particular concern with the preparation of young black people for dealing with racism and resolving issues of identity and culture, and there is a growing concern about sexist attitudes towards young women (Robson, 1987). Another factor leading to success may well be the provision of carefully thought out adult resources and supervision. If foster adolescents' self-help groups are to succeed they will require the same factors to be considered.

Mentor/befriending

Another approach involves the use of volunteer mentors or befrienders, to help young people in the transition from care to independent status. An example is that of the Orphan Foundation (Newsletter, 1986; Rowe, 1983b) which describes leaving foster care as a 'second orphaning'.

Following the model of Big Brother and Big Sister programs, the Orphan Foundation's volunteers undergo training before assignment to a youth and continue to receive training during participation. The youth and volunteer, prior to discharge from care, receive training in:

- individualized goal planning;
- independent household living;
- career development;
- job search;
- maintaining employment;
- consumer economics;
- health care;
- recreation.

Following completion of training, the volunteers are assigned to individual youths. This assignment pre-dates discharge from care, so as to encourage a relationship that can survive the changes in the youth's life styles and locales. After discharge from care, the Orphan Foundation regularly contacts the youth and volunteers to see how their relationship is enduring and to offer help if necessary. Volunteers receive continuing education and refresher courses. Groups and counseling are offered to the youth. No systematic evaluations of similar programs are available, but numerous replications of the Orphan Foundation's approach suggests its significant promise. An organization in the UK, which parallels the Orphan Foundation in some ways, is the National Association of Young People in Care (NAYPIC), run by young people formerly in care, which provides support for those in care and acts as a pressure group on central government and social services.

Employment services

Employment experiences and skills are crucial to the stabilization of interdependent living arrangements for foster adolescents. Probably every emancipation contract between social workers and youth includes some agreement about obtaining a job skill or a job. Typical residential emancipation programs require that participants attend a job preparation program and then complete a job search program. Residents are also usually required to have a job within two weeks; after that they can look for a better position. Youths are expected to put aside the bulk of their earnings and to save a considerable nest egg before discharge.

Since most emancipating youth are not in special residences, other strategies are needed to promote job finding and keeping. 'Job Opportunities For Youth' (JOY) is a project to develop stronger linkages between runaway and homeless youth, many of whom come from foster care, and service providers and state employment and training programs in the New England area (Johnson and Nelson 1986). JOY has established a 'regional network' that meets three times a year and helps co-ordinate the activities of local networks through technical assistance, a clearing house, staff support, and meetings. Despite the modest success of collaboration, referrals to state job training programs have not been great in number. Difficulties in collaboration as well as alternative programs available for foster youth have left little incentive to continue the networks. For example, there are few job training programs for in-school youth during the school year. Moreover, out of school youth have to support themselves with job training wages, which are not competitive with other private employers.

Despite the mixed results of the above programs, job development and employment training appears to be the key to successful interdependent living. In a survey of 42 providers of services to adolescents in the San Francisco area, nearly three-quarters of providers nominated employment as the most pressing need of adolescents who were recently or soon to be discharged from care. Similarly, the study by Stein and Carey (1986) in England found that young people who had left care were poorly equipped for employment.

Intensive case co-ordination

In the US, interdependent living services for young people generally do not have a specific physical site, but instead are in the hearts and routines of social workers with specialized caseloads. As the following programs show, intensive case coordination is required for maximum effectiveness in many programs. Examples include the Independent Living Program of Ville Marie Social Service Center in Montreal, which retains a social worker to work with a caseload of 20 young persons who are approaching discharge.

Another example is Project Independence, operated by the Children's Home Society of Winnipeg in Manitoba, Canada, which employs a client-specific model that includes ongoing home visits, life planning meetings and monitoring of living accommodation. The intensity of the social work-client contact may vary from weekly to daily and the levels of residential supervision range from living alone in an apartment to living in a two-person apartment with a 'proctor', another young person who is employed part-time or attending college, and who is paid either half or full-time salary. The proctor is supervised by the social worker and is involved in teaching the full range of life skills and in helping the client develop a positive social network and community contacts. The basic service involves weekly home visits and meetings with youths; this is supplemented by other resources as needed, including help finding a residence or job, basic life skills assessment and training, and meeting with significant others. Also available for clients who need additional monitoring and support are daily home visits, structured evening leisure activities twice each week with one-on-one involvement, assistance in structuring weekend leisure time, and 24-hour worker accessibility. The Children's Home Society contracts with other agencies in child welfare, mental health and juvenile justice to provide these services.

As with the above project, many emancipation programs provide more than one form of service. For example, Project Stepping Out begins with an assessment of the strengths and needs of each youth (Pasztor, Clarren, Timberlake, and Bayless, 1986). The program offers young people all-day workshops on various skills; task-centerd groups; apprenticeships and summer jobs to provide 'hands-on' employment experience; volunteers to serve as adult role models; and remedial services. Even though the project's combination of resources has been modestly effective, the obstacles encountered have taken much time and energy to overcome. For instance, there have been problems in arranging apprenticeships, obtaining volunteers, and getting youths to attend workshops. The authors highlight several lessons learned in carrying out this program:

– concentrate on solving community liaison problems;
– ensure that foster parents know the developmental needs of teens and how to support the adolescent's growth toward self-sufficiency;
– work with the youth earlier in the foster care experience;
– offer supportive and rehabilitative services for birth families, to facilitate their serving as support networks later;
– provide transitional funding for youths in foster care, to meet basic needs and allow them to build resources toward the future.

(Pasztor, Clarren, Timberlake, and Bayliss, 1986)

IMPLICATIONS FOR POLICY AND PRACTICE

Although there has been limited empirical evaluation of the programs reviewed in this chapter, some implications for policy and practice are suggested. First, the limited appeal of group homes, as presently designed, is becoming clearer. The recognition seems to be provoking a more flexible, shorter-term model that may ultimately look more like a residential version of a support group. Whatever their form, such programs have a key contribution to make in helping youth avoid homelessness and the threats to health of body and mind that it entails.

Independent living subsidy programs provide the greatest flexibility and move young people in care the closest to being self-sufficient without cutting the cord to the agency. The proliferation of these programs is in some doubt, however, because of insurance concerns and because they are not reimbursable under current federal regulations in the US. The promising finding from the previously mentioned Oregon project (Halm, 1980) is that these programs are not only successful for youth with the most skill and responsibility, but also for the higher risk youth for whom they are designed. The subsidy concept can be integrated in part into group homes and foster family care, by turning checks over to youth for their use as soon as they appear able to resist grossly misusing them.

Mentor and self-help programs can complement residential preparation. The involvement of people who can assume some of the roles of family and be available at the crisis points can be invaluable. The concept is supported by respondents in Festinger's (1983) study, who identified the need for groups in which foster care 'graduates' visit and counsel with soon-to-be discharged foster children. With encouragement and consultation from child welfare agencies, civic and religious organizations can serve as a source of mentors or, as a group, help youth to acquire household furnishings, find work, and establish a supportive social network.

Education and employment programs must coexist. Young people in foster care without basic education will find little success in programs like the Job Training and Partnership Act in the US, which is known for serving the most able of the unemployed. Employment services seem to be the most promising and least explored aspect of preparation for interdependent living. These services must be buttressed by special compensatory and education services. Even when special programs cannot be established, the assignment of contact teachers or administrators for youth served under social services seems to give young people much needed support.

Co-ordinated education and employment programs have an enormous appeal for youth needing assistance making the transition to adulthood (Brindis, Barth, and Loomis, 1987). The opportunity to meet

137

with a job counselor is a great enticement for young people. Unfortunately social services and employment services have often been separate. Residential programs and agencies serving adolescents in foster care could team to develop their own job clubs and job search activities. Job developers may be the most important resource; they have succeeded well with other hard-to-employ populations.

Regardless of the form of an independent living program, the key ingredient may well be case co-ordination. Special adolescent caseloads with lower numbers of clients can provide the continuity across these programs and resources that youth will need. The previously described program of the Children's Home Society of Winnipeg models the best of this approach. Similarly, in the UK, Shaw and Hipgrave have drawn attention to the value of specialist teams 'which would normally comprise specialist field staff, residential social workers, foster parents and team leader'. (Shaw and Hipgrave, 1983, p. 118). In the Winnipeg program, youths get considerable assistance in identifying what resources they need and in developing arrangements for their attainment. Of course, the more options there are the better the case co-ordinator can orchestrate services. Regardless of currently available resources, social workers could assume specialized caseloads for foster care youth in virtually every child welfare agency, and use social work skills to develop additional informal and formal resources.

CONCLUSION

Development of effective programs for adolescents in foster family care requires an ecological perspective beginning at the broadest level of influence. Laws need amending both in the US and the UK, to extend the opportunity for financial assistance to age 21 for foster adolescents who continue to pursue academic and vocational goals. Implementation of permanency planning regulations so that more youth are adopted will lessen the numbers of children who grow up in foster care (Barth and Berry, 1988). Additionally, greater emphasis on maintaining links between families and young people in care will leave fewer young people to address the challenge of adulthood without reliance on a family. Furthermore, there should be far more attention paid to the educational needs of young people in foster family care, beginning at the point of entry. Finally, to identify what are the most successful programs, service activities and client outcomes need to be assessed more rigorously.

9 *Thinking about assessment of foster parents*

Martin Shaw

Like other areas of child welfare, foster family care has its share of critical decision points – whether, when and where to place a child, or to terminate a placement, how (if at all) to involve birth parents, and so on – all of which have profound implications for the futures of all parties concerned. Of these decision points in the UK, probably none has been more discussed than the assessment of foster parents: in the words of George, researchers and practitioners 'have spent a great deal more time discussing the initial assessment of foster parents than how to help, guide and supervise them after the child is placed with them' (George, 1970, p. 92). The balance of interest may have shifted somewhat since these words were written, but foster parent assessment remains a key issue in foster care practice. This chapter looks at how assessment has been thought of at different times and raises questions as to possible future lines of development.

Although the focus of this chapter is on *how* to assess, there is an important prior question of *what* to assess – what are the qualities necessary in foster parents who are to work with adolescents? The most frequent response to this question is a list of characteristics that are doubtless desirable but tend towards the grandiose – maturity, self-awareness, understanding, and so on – raising doubts as to whether we are seeking foster parents or recruits to the heavenly choir.

At a more human level, the characteristics which Katz has found to be associated with success in older-child adoptions may well have relevance to the fostering of adolescents; parents' tolerance of their own ambivalent feelings; refusal to be rejected by the child; ability to delay their own gratification and to find happiness in small increments of improvement; role flexibility; a firm sense of entitlement or certainty that the child is a family member (is this a virtue or a vice in fostering as against adoption?); what she describes as 'intrusive' and controlling qualities, exercised in a caring way; humour and self-care; and an open rather than closed family system (Katz, 1986). Some remarkably similar qualities were noted in another recent study, again in the field of adoption: the confidence of the adoptive parents that they would not follow through on their destructive impulses towards the young people; and humour and 'creative discipline' on the part of the adoptive fathers (Kagan and Reid, 1986). There appears to be little equivalent recent research in the fostering field where, as will become clear later in this chapter, the switch of focus in family assessment from content to process – from what to assess to how to assess – has if anything been even more marked than in adoption. An exception is a study by Cautley (1980), who concluded that there is a range of characteristics 'most predictive' of successful foster parents, in such areas as familiarity with children, parenting skills, decision-making patterns within the family and attitudes to parenting.

AN HISTORICAL PERSPECTIVE

We still lack a comprehensive history of foster family care but several writers, such as George in the UK and Wolins in the US, offer fascinating glimpses into earlier thinking (George, 1970, 1971; Wolins, 1963). Both writers give prominence to the 1874/75 Report to the English Local Government Board in which the Inspector, Mr Bowyer, put his finger on the basic weakness of the 'boarding out' system, namely that it is founded on two opposing principles: 'confidence in the benevolence of human nature' and 'distrust of its selfishness and dishonesty'.

Confidence and distrust are well demonstrated in the work of the late nineteenth-century American pioneers, Brace and Birtwell. Brace, a minister of religion reputed to have placed 75,000 children in foster homes in the West, assumed that only good Christian families took children into their care and that there was therefore no need for investigation. Birtwell was convinced of the importance of foster home investigation focusing on specific attributes of the family and its home, such as the character of each family member, the distance to church and school, previous child care experience, space available for the foster child, and plans for integrating the child into the household (Wolins, 1963).

An English local government board report of the same period (1880) divided foster homes into five groups according to the foster parents' reasons for taking the child: those who were childless but could not afford to adopt; those taking a child 'from real charity and pity for an orphan'; those fostering for profit (interestingly, this motive was acceptable if readily admitted); those wishing to train the child as a servant (a motive generally considered unsatisfactory); and those with mixed motives which were difficult to assess. An approved foster home was considered suitable for any child of a particular age and sex, and it was not uncommon for 'matching' to be done by drawing lots (George, 1970).

The Curtis Report of 1946, which was specifically concerned with children in care in England and Wales and was to have a profound effect on the direction of child welfare for many years, came down strongly in favour of foster family care, but was nonetheless critical of much of the fostering practice that the committee members had examined. Those responsible for selecting and supervising foster homes, whether paid officials or voluntary visitors, generally had neither the experience nor the training necessary for the work, and the committee reported a sizeable 'hit or miss' element in foster home investigation. The Curtis Report led to the establishment of a more comprehensive service for children in care and to the setting up of training courses for social workers involved in child care work. (For a fuller historical account of these developments, see Packman 1981).

Because of the dearth of home-grown literature, child care training courses in the UK were for some years largely dependent on US material. There is room for debate as to whether the so-called 'psychiatric deluge' was as powerful an influence on UK social work practice generally as had long been supposed (Yelloly, 1980), but the standard texts on child welfare, particularly foster care and adoption, were overwhelmingly psycho-dynamic in approach. As a consequence, in the area of foster home assessment, much attention centred on the motivation, especially the unconscious motivation, of prospective foster parents. As early as 1952, Towle warned against a simplistic over-emphasis on this aspect, pointing out that, while some motives are promising and others suspect, 'there is no such thing as a good or bad motive in and of itself'. Motives could not be evaluated out of context. Most important of all was the fallacy of thinking that to know the motive was to know the outcome of a course of action (Towle, 1952).

Despite Towle's cautionary article, child care workers engaged vigorously in the game of 'Hunt the Pathology'. Starting from the basic assumption that people apply to foster in order to solve some problem of their own (Stone, 1967), the main task of the social worker was to strip away the layers of 'good' motives until the 'real' (i.e. bad) motive lay revealed. Kay reported a psychiatrist's view that a principal motive for fostering was the wish to avoid breast feeding (Kay, 1966), and the present writer, who first practised in the early 1960s, retains vivid memories of the sinister interpretations imposed on the stated wishes of fostering applicants: those who sought to foster babies short-term were people who could not tolerate the idea of infants becoming less dependent; those who asked for a toddler might be denying the primitive parts of their psyche which a baby might evoke; willingness to foster an even mildly handicapped child was evidence of poor self-image; and so on. Foster parent applicants were suspected of lacking sufficient commitment to adopt, whilst adoptive applicants were probably over-possessive. The logic of this approach is that no one should have been allowed to foster at all. However, given that foster homes were needed, the realistic option was to 'approve' some but never trust them an inch.

Closely allied to the 'motivation' approach was that which paid primary attention to foster parents' needs, again unconscious as much as conscious. Kay, for example, identified two patterns of need in successful long-term foster parents: those who urgently desired a child of their own but were unwilling or unable to conceive one and those who identified strongly with deprived or unhappy children because of memories of deprivation in their own childhood (Kay, 1966). Unfortunately, need (like motive) has proved to be an elusive concept and no predictor of success in the fostering enterprise. The extent to which thinking on foster home assessment derived from the world of clinical psychiatry is also seen in a paper advocating the use of Rorschach tests on foster parent applicants (Holman, 1964). It is hardly surprising that many applicants found the assessment process (or 'vetting', as it was often called) to be a confusing, alienating experience – an examination on an unstated curriculum for which it was impossible to learn the 'correct' answers. The social worker role in 'vetting' was that of inquisitor, detached from and superior to the applicants (supplicants?), probing and waiting to catch them out in a wrong answer or suspect motive.

An alternative approach, proposed by Trasler, encouraged foster parents to look to the future rather than the past, and to consider whether their expectations of any foster child placed were sufficiently open, flexible and realistic to allow the child to be happily accommodated in their lives (Trasler, 1960). This approach, forward looking in more senses than one, contained elements of what we would now call 'preparation' and has clear links with current trends in assessment.

It is, of course, possible to pathologize the future, and it was not uncommon for social workers to present applicants with a horrific picture of life with foster children – foul language, smearing faeces on the bathroom walls, engaging in delinquent behaviour in the neighbourhood and in unnatural practices with the family pet – so as to frighten off 'unsuitable' applicants. To provide added realism, these descriptions might omit any suggestion that foster parents were to be provided with skills or offered help from a visting social worker to deal with behaviour problems in their foster children. Whilst it is necessary to dispel rosy illusions, this procedure seemed designed to freeze out all but the most dedicated or incorrigibly masochistic of applicants, leaving perhaps only those with an 'unconscious need' to be visited by sadistic social workers.

By the late 1960s and early 1970s, traditional approaches to foster home assessment were under attack on a number of fronts. The exploration of motivation had proved difficult and unrewarding, satisfactory motives being no guarantee of satisfactory performance (Towle, 1952). More generally, there was questioning of the appropriateness of quasi-therapeutic approaches to people offering a service rather than seeking help. Criticism of psychodynamic approaches was encouraging the exploration of alternative models of behaviour from psychology, particularly behavioural and cognitive theories, and from sociology, role theory and systems being seen as fruitful areas of study. It was coming to be recognized also that social workers' assessments often said as much about their own values as they did about the applicants. Wolins' research had shown social workers' images of the ideal foster parent to bear an uncanny resemblance to the social workers themselves (Wolins, 1963). That this situation still holds true is indicated by a more recent UK study in which social workers showed themselves inclined to prefer as foster parents people like themselves in terms of attitude and life style (McWhinnie, 1980).

RECENT DEVELOPMENTS

During recent years, increasing criticism has been directed not so much at specific assessment criteria as at the emphasis given to assessment, and to the value of an assessment approach per se in foster family placement work (Wiehe, 1977; Hartman, 1979; Smith, 1984). Considerable research effort has failed to identify any set of factors by which the effectiveness or otherwise of particular foster parents can be predicted. The main message seems to be that success or failure is determined more by factors arising during the placement than by the applicants' previous history (Kadushin, 1971). Social workers may have the skills to screen out grossly unsuitable applicants but not to discriminate amongst those who fall within a broadly 'normal' range. The assessment approach has also been criticized for setting up a high degree of dependency on the part of the applicants, which is likely to be counter-productive at a later stage when a more collaborative relationship is called for between foster parents and social worker.

Wiehe is particularly critical of the fact that the apparatus of assessment is geared to those not suitable for fostering – a small percentage of the applicants who follow through after the initial screening process – and that good applicants benefit little from the assessment study (Wiehe, 1977). Knowing that they are being assessed, applicants become more concerned with making a good impression and thinking of the 'correct' answers than with learning about, or exploring for themselves their suitability for, fostering. The ineffectiveness of traditional assessment methods was, for some social workers, brought home most forcibly in their attempts to recruit families for ethnic minority children. In the 1975/76 Soul Kids Campaign in London, the question was raised as to whether Afro-Caribbean applicants 'needed a more personal, less bureaucratic approach when they applied to foster or adopt'. The Steering Group reported that the question was not fully tested but 'the overall impression was that any modifications that might be introduced to make application processes less formal, less lengthy and less apparently prying would be welcomed as much by whites as by blacks' (Association of British Adoption Agencies, 1977, p. 17).

Criticisms of this kind have gained added force in recent years with the rapid development and expansion of foster parent roles and tasks. Earlier thinking and practice were based on a comparatively narrow view of the foster parent function as being to care for the child on a short- or long-term basis while others in the foster care system engaged in any necessary therapeutic work with the child or birth parents. Ryan, McFadden and Warren (1981) draw attention to the need for a range of foster care provision to meet the requirements of different situations: child-oriented foster care; foster parents supportive of biological relationships; and foster parents positively oriented towards the birth family. With the growth of permanency thinking (Maluccio, Fein and Olmstead, 1986) and the greatly increased proportion of adolescents being considered for family placement, the demand for purely child-oriented foster homes is likely to diminish, with a corresponding increase in the need for foster parents able to develop a wide set of roles; as parent counsellors (Johnston and Gabor, 1981), parent aides (Seaberg, 1981), role models (Davis and Bland, 1981), as well as key workers for the child or young person (Dubois and Mockler, 1984). The potential for foster parent involvement with adolescents and their families has been discussed elsewhere (Shaw and Hipgrave, 1983; and Chapters 6 and 10).

NEW ASSUMPTIONS ABOUT ASSESSMENT

In the changing world of family placement, foster care has recently developed a new set of working assumptions in relation to assessment of foster parents for adolescents, which are equally applicable to children of other ages. These may be summarized as follows:

1 Fostering family care is a term embracing not one but many roles, differing in their aims and thus in the skills required.
2 Fostering theory, derived largely from experience with young children, needs substantial rethinking before being applied to adolescents.
3 Foster care knowledge and expertise do not lie exclusively with any one party to the system – birth parents and relatives, young people, foster parents and social workers all have a contribution to make to the success or failure of the enterprise. Collaboration which ensures that all parties are involved is the key to effective foster care practice.
4 Given the range of roles and tasks in fostering, there can be no uniform set of criteria of 'suitability' for foster parents.
5 Scope for prediction is severely limited and the major effort must go into preparation, training and on-the-job consultation and help for foster parents.
6 Foster parent applicants come to the agency, in the main, as mature and competent people offering their skills in partnership with the agency – there should be nothing in the agency's response at any stage which might de-skill or induce unhealthy dependence in the foster parents.

The underlying message that there are now no certainties and that they can no longer be in sole charge affects social workers in various ways. Many are responding to the challenge and are working out the implications of this new thinking with their foster parent colleagues. (See Maluccio, Krieger and Pine, in press). Release from previous received wisdom has had a liberating effect – perhaps the major challenge for social workers is to avoid becoming prisoners of the new received wisdom!

MODELS OF SELECTION

The reluctance of others to move beyond old-style vetting, despite all the evidence as to its ineffectiveness, is worth exploring for a moment. It is tempting to conclude that vetting persists because it gives its practitioners something to do, seems to justify their existence, and establishes their position of centrality and dominance in the foster care system from the outset.

Another possible reaction to the above list of assumptions is simply to book a suitable meeting-place, organize refreshments, and leave applicants to get on with selecting themselves. Part of the attraction of this option is that it seems to offer scope for widening the working definitions of 'suitability' within which social workers, however liberal their intentions, operate. Whether applicants or the general public would be less conservative in their choice of foster parents may well be an illusion – certainly, agencies have met with some resistance from their lay committees (or governing bodies) in recent years when attempting to broaden selection to include, for example, single parents or gay and lesbian applicants.

It is doubtful whether self-selection has been or ever can be employed in anything like a pure form, as it would be regarded as an abdication of responsibility by the professional staff. The notion that, given adequate information, people are capable of learning for themselves if and when they are ready to foster does not deal adequately with at least two groups: those who may need a gentle push to overcome residual doubts in the face of the complexity of the fostering task; and those who lack the self-awareness to see that they lack the capacity to be effective foster parents.

The use of a group approach has some clear advantages over individual interview methods, including:

- reducing professional distance between social workers and applicants;
- offering opportunities for applicants to support and learn from one another and from experienced foster parents;
- the linking of assessment to preparation and training.

It is of course quite possible to generate a 'vetting' atmosphere in a group, leaving applicants as uncertain and dependent on the worker as in one-to-one interviews. Much depends upon the attitudes and skills of social workers in establishing a comfortable climate in which group members may share uncertainties as well as information and ideas. Similarly, it is important to clarify the function of the group at different stages – is it for assessment? for preparation? – if the problem of 'examination on a concealed curriculum' is to be avoided.

Whether individual or group methods (or both) are employed, there remains a proper role for social workers in giving information and in helping applicants explore their potential for the tasks of family placement. Certain techniques of diagrammatic assessment – particularly the ecomap and geneogram advocated by Hartman (Hartman, 1979; Hartman and Laird, 1983) – seem particularly suited to the more open, cooperative and egalitarian approach which many practitioners are now seeking. Similarly, methods geared to the joint identification of foster care tasks and the applicants' likely responses are being developed (Davis, Morris, and Thorn 1984). If we can only renounce the fruitless quest for the magic ingredient which makes a successful foster parent, research may still offer social workers some useful guidelines in this area (Shaw, 1986).

LOOKING AHEAD

Looking ahead from our present position, there remains the problem posed at the beginning of this chapter: the contradictory nature of our attitudes to foster parents – do we really trust them or not? Some years ago, writing from his experience in the world of industry, McGregor identified two theories of human motivation which have some relevance to foster home care, and indeed to other areas of social work. Briefly, Theory X assumes that people dislike work and will avoid it if possible; that they must be controlled, coerced and directed in order to make them work; and that most people prefer to be dealt with in this fashion rather than have to carry responsibility or exercise initiative. Theory Y assumes that, for most of us, work is as natural as play; that control and punishment are not the only ways to achieve organizational objectives; and that people exercise self-control, self-direction, imagination and initiative to achieve objectives to which they are committed (McGregor, 1960).

Strategies of management and supervision based on trust or distrust are self-reinforcing (Pym, 1968). Strategies based on distrust involve interfering with people's work, withholding information, and demanding excessive information, and result in people feeling undervalued. Conversely, strategies of trust involve delegation and maximizing the downward flow of information, and enhance job satisfaction. The implications of those ideas go way beyond the terms of reference of this chapter – how foster homes should be supervised, whether social workers can apply strategies of trust in their dealings with foster parents when they themselves are subject to strategies of distrust by their own management, and so on. For the present discussion, it is worth noting that these assumptions about behaviour cast their shadows forward in the foster care process, to the point at which social workers first encounter people who offer themselves as foster parents.

When thinking about assessment, it is also important to bear in mind the issue of power. Although in some sense we are all continually assessing one another, the assessment that carries weight is that conducted by the most powerful members of a system in relation to those who are weaker – typically workers assess clients, social work teachers assess students, and social workers assess foster parents. As foster parents continue to gain expertise and status, it would be reasonable to expect that in time some of the significant assessment activity will flow in the reverse direction .

It is also important to note that a recurrent and frustrating feature of evaluative research in social work is that it generally ignores, as being too difficult to measure, the behaviour of social workers themselves. Researchers concentrate their attention on a method of intervention, or on the characteristics of other actors in the drama, such as foster parents, birth parents and children. In a recent study of task-centred casework, for example, the authors commented that some social workers were clearly better than others at applying the method. However, these variations in competence were not examined in any way that could be incorporated into the final evaluation (Goldberg, Gibbons, and Sinclair, 1985).

If the quality of social workers' performance is ignored, there is a strong likelihood that a method will be blamed for deficiencies in some of the workers. Everyday observation indicates that some social workers are better at some things than others are; and that their impact on people ranges from the psycho-therapeutic to the psycho-noxious. Foster parents on the receiving end recognize that, if there is social work help, there is also social work hindrance. No social worker can expect to be good at everything, and it is perhaps time to study the qualities and behaviour which are conducive to effective foster care practice by social workers. In this process, other parties in the foster care system would be necessary contributors, and foster parents would be less than human if, initially at least, they did not relish the thought of inflicting some traditional modes of assessment on their prospective social workers. A vetting approach, perhaps, might come to mind. ('Tell us something about your relationship with your supervisor'); or a task-centred approach ('One of your tasks will be to respond to crises at times inconvenient to yourself, like 5.00 p.m. on a Friday – do you think you are ready for this yet?') Or perhaps, given their essential humanity, foster parents will simply settle for an educational approach to their social workers.

A greater challenge may lie ahead if we take on board the full implications of the idea outlined in Chapter 2, that foster care is a social system (see also Eastman, 1979). We know from the field of family therapy, for example, that we cannot understand the behaviour of any one member, or indeed all the members, by studying each of them in isolation. Each member's behaviour is in large measure the product of their interaction with the others. Again, impressionistically, we know that some foster parents work best with some kinds of children, some social workers do better with certain foster parents, and so on. What this seems to cry out for is what we might call systems assessment or evaluation – how effectively is this system meeting the needs of the foster child or adolescent? How can each member of this system, including birth parents, best help the others to make their contribution most effectively? What are the implications of a systems perspective for assessment of foster families for adolescents?

CONCLUSION

This chapter has highlighted a number of points which are important in the assessment of foster families:

1 Approaches to foster home assessment over the years have been characterized by social workers' (and society's) ambivalent attitudes – confidence versus distrust – towards foster parents themselves.
2 Principles of assessment derived from clinical practice with clients' presenting problems should not be employed in unmodified form on people interested in providing a service.
3 Motivation is neither an indicator of suitability nor a guarantee of performance.
4 An over-emphasis on assessment diverts energy that could more usefully be applied to preparation, and establishes an unhelpful model for the future working relationship between social worker and foster parents.
5 The changing world of family placement or foster care practice, as it

is now more commonly known, in which the old rules do not apply and social workers are not the sole experts, has necessitated fundamental rethinking of the roles and tasks of the various parties involved.

6 In attempting to assess the actual or potential effectiveness of a foster family, it will be more fruitful (if more difficult) to apply a systems perspective than to study the personal characteristics of any one of the participants.

If we can begin to look at how different sorts of contribution mesh together to achieve the overall aims, we may be less inclined to scapegoat individuals for failing in the system, and more inclined to work collaboratively towards a common goal. Using a systems framework, we see why the question 'What makes a good foster parent?' has never been, and never can be, satisfactorily answered. As well as foster parents' own characteristics and behaviour, social workers, foster children and birth parents have a contribution to the making (or unmaking) of an effective foster parent. Framing assessment and related issues in systems terms also shows us what a long way we have to go. Perhaps, given the complexity and possible permutations of our various interactions, we never shall produce all the answers but we can make a start by asking ourselves better questions.

10 The training of foster parents for work with adolescents

Barbara A. Pine and Marc Jacobs

Training prepares people to perform tasks and functions related to work that they have been selected to do, usually in relation to some expected outcome such as the achievement of a level of performance or competence which ensures that the individual is contributing to the accomplishment of an organization's goals. Implicit in this notion of training are a certain clarity of both organizational purpose and the individual's role in attaining it, some consensus about the requisite knowledge, skills and attitudes for performing that role and, perhaps most importantly, an understanding of the limits as well as the potential of training as one component of a generally complex work system.

This chapter sets these principles in the context of the training of foster parents to be caregivers to adolescents. In keeping with the above definition, foster parent training is viewed both broadly – as one part of the dynamic complex of foster care services – and with a more narrow focus on ideas and content linked to foster parenting roles. Following a brief discussion of permanency planning and interdependent living, the chapter consists of two main sections:

1 A review of more recent perceptions of foster parent roles as they are reflected in various US training materials, along with brief descriptions of selected curricula, to assist trainers by identifying some of the generic, as well as specific, content contained in some of the training resources currently available; and
2 Discussion of issues and guidelines in the training of foster parents to prepare adolescents for self-sufficiency.

151

BACKGROUND

Permanency planning and foster family care

Recent and radical changes in child welfare policy and practice have dramatically influenced the foster care system. These reform efforts, called collectively permanency planning, have resulted in new outcomes for service and new roles for foster parents in providing these services to dependent children and their families. A similar expansion of foster parent roles has taken place in the UK (Rowe, 1983a; Clarkson and Whistlecraft, 1987). In both countries, foster parents have become 'partners in permanency planning' with the aims of effecting re-unification with birth parents, preparing children for adoptive place-ments, providing permanent shared care for older children or, increasingly, offering more specialist foster care, embracing assessment and treatment models (see, for example, Shaw and Hipgrave, 1983; Snodgrass and Bryant, in press).

As noted in Chapter 1, the relative success, over the past ten years, of implementing permanency planning in the US has resulted in a much older population of children in care, as fewer younger children entered the system and those who did stayed for shorter periods of time. To some extent this trend has also been reflected in the UK. As indicated in Chapter 1, in both countries adolescents now comprise over 50 per cent of children in care.

Interdependent living

The special needs of these children present major challenges for the foster care system. In addition to a continued focus on foster parents as role models for youth, as advocates helping youth develop needed community and social supports, as team members for case planning and review and as supporters of birth families, foster parents of adolescents have an additional role to prepare adolescents for 'interdependent living', a concept that was introduced in Chapters 1 and 4. But how can we achieve this concept in practice? What is the set of skills required to promote greater 'concrete' self-sufficiency and also contribute to a youth's development of the type of positive self-concept and identity necessary for building productive relationships with family members, peers, associates in the workplace, and other adults in the community? How can young people, many seen as socially and emotionally isolated, be helped to develop the supportive network of relationships involved in living *interdependently* with others? And, what resources are available to support foster parents whose main role is to prepare youth for interdependent living?

One useful way of cataloging and organizing the various skills that young people require to become competent adults is provided by the design of a recent US survey of adolescent emancipation programs (Cook and Ansell, 1986). This survey delineated skills in two major areas – tangible and intangible:

Tangible skills	*Intangible skills*
Education	Social skills
Job readiness and training	Communication skills
Use of transportation	Decision-making
Money management	Problem-solving
Locating housing	Interpersonal relations planning
Health care	Preparing for the transition to
Shopping and cooking	independence from substitute
Locating and using community	care
resources	Confronting anger and past losses
Consumer skills	and rejections
Understanding the law	Interpersonal relationships
	(Cook and Ansell, 1986, p. 3.1)

Achievement in each of these areas is crucial to meeting inter-dependent living goals. The framework of tangible and intangible skills mirrors the findings of similar studies in the UK (Godek, 1976; Porter, 1983; Stein and Carey, 1986). Such a framework provides a useful backdrop to the following brief review of selected foster parent training resources, some of which are focused on the more generic aspects of foster parenting, and others on the particular issues involved in helping youth develop the skills needed for successful transition to adulthood.

A LOOK AT SELECTED CURRICULUM RESOURCES

Earlier curricula

A variety of curricula on fostering adolescents was developed, during the mid- and late-1970s, promoting the idea of foster parents as partners within the care team. This philosophy, now known collectively as the parenting plus approach, is reflected in general training material for foster parents both in the UK and the US. These curricula are described concisely below:

Foster Parenting an Adolescent – Child Welfare League of America (1977) and (reprint) National Foster Care Association UK (1982)
The course consists of seven 2–3 hour sessions on the following topics: adolescent behavior, adolescent development; listening and responding; ways of getting along; adolescent life tasks; relationships and personal identity. The course attempts to identify typical situations that may arise and includes a combination of information sharing with an exploration of feelings and responses to parenting a teenager.

Fostering the Teenager – Loppnow (1978) – Eastern Michigan University
This was developed for the Foster Parent Training Project of Eastern Michigan University. It is a ten-session course which includes topics such as identifying rewards and problems in fostering teenagers; the teenage years as a stage of development; use of community resources; running away; alcohol and other drugs; and sexual acting out. Three sessions are included on living together in families, with topics such as personal hygiene and self-maintenance; chores, earning money and sharing property; discipline, obedience, and sassiness or cheekiness. The course provides a basic foundation for parenting the foster adolescent.

While the above manuals are helpful in identifying what might be expected from adolescents and how foster families might respond in specific circumstances, there has been a dearth of training for foster parents on the concepts and techniques involved in implementing permanency planning for adolescents in general (Pasztor, 1985). The following curriculum models have attempted to address this problem.

Preparation for Fostering: Pre-service Education for Foster Families – Pasztor (1983) – Nova University
The Nova model combines foster parent pre-service training with the home study process. It was the first comprehensive, preparatory training program that emphasized both foster parents' critical role as team members and permanency planning goals. It is based on shared decision-making, problem-solving and mutual selection. An important feature is that foster parents write most of their own home studies, which are structured to help them assess the impact of fostering on their family. The written material and home visits from workers allow both to make an informed assessment about their ability to work together.

A further feature of the Nova model is that a foster parent/social worker team leads the training (as in the National Foster Care Association's training material in the UK). Foster parents are able to assess their own strengths and limits through sets of problem-solving, skill-focused experiential activities. Significantly, this approach requires the foster care agency to come to its own understanding of the role of foster parents in the delivery of services. Selection and training of foster parents are viewed in context of the agency's overall foster care program, contributing to greater congruence between program goals and the services delivered as well as placing training in a clearer relationship to the overall foster care program of the agency.

MAPP: Model Approach to Partnership in Parenting – Pasztor (1986) – National Center for Foster and Residential Care
This is a structured and entirely scripted pre-service training and mutual assessment model that supports the partnership between foster parent and agencies to meet permanency planning goals. It aims to prepare members for the many feelings and emotions that will arise from their foster care experience. Family assessment and preparation components are combined.

MAPP reflects the ecological perspective of working with families and children (see Chapter 1) because it is designed to reaffirm the inherent strengths and resources of some families; provide a process for helping families develop their strengths, resources and potential to be successful foster families, and help some families to select out of the program.

Training Foster Parents of Adolescents – Brin, Pilowy, Wallace, Wasson and Wolf (1985) – New York State Child Welfare Training Institute. State University College at Buffalo
This training pack addresses a wide range of caregiving tasks, permanency planning tasks, and special care issues involved in fostering the adolescent. With over 70 hours of training materials, this curriculum demonstrates the complexity of working with challenging adolescents. Stressing the 'parenting plus' role of foster parents, there are extensive materials relating to adolescent development, including sexual development, the importance of self-concept, and the use of discipline to enhance development.

Several units address some of the permanency planning tasks of the fostering role, including adoption and work with birth families to achieve reunification. Another unit considers the preparation of adolescents for interdependent living. It is one of the first units to concentrate on the process of preparation with the youngster and look toward the development of the supportive networks that young people so critically need.

There are two additional resources focusing on work with adolescents that can be adapted for foster parent training.

Making It On Your Own (Ansell, 1983)
This resource has the particular advantage of being in the form of a workbook that provides a structure for a youngster to move at his/her own pace. It allows the youth to work alone, with others in a group, or with the aid of caregivers.

The Road to Independent Living (Bayless, 1986)
This approach concentrates on providing support to foster parents and detailed guidance on how to plan activities with teenagers, with the aim of developing both tangible and intangible skills.

Newly developed curricula

The following curricula are the most current. Also, they incorporate the best features of earlier works and focus on preparation of young people in care for interdependent living.

PUSH/GOALS – Ryan (1987) – Eastern Michigan University
This is a 50 hour, four-module curriculum for foster parents, with companion materials for use with adolescents, that has been developed at the Institute for the Study of Children and Families at Eastern Michigan University. PUSH ('Providing Understanding, Support, and Help for Youth') provides foster parents with guidance for the use of GOALS ('Going Out and Living Successfully') materials with their foster youth. The materials are designed for flexible use and, since they focus on the foster parent as the primary teacher, allow for an individualized program for adolescents of varying abilities.

Intangible skills, such as decision-making, building self-esteem and understanding emotional responses, are emphasized in the two modules entitled 'choices and consequences' and 'leaving home again', while the more tangible skills needed for independence are the focus of the two modules entitled 'self-help skills' and 'employability'.

The developers of this curriculum have tested it by using parallel youth and foster parent groups. The youth groups have been so successful in setting the stage for the adolescents' work on GOALS with their foster parents that a manual on leading similar groups is being written for agencies that can take this optional approach.

Another unique feature of this material is that it can be used over a longer term, beginning with younger adolescents. For example, foster parents could introduce the 'self-help skills' to a 14-year-old, move into 'choices and consequences' the following year, and by the time the youth was 17 years old, work on exercises in the last module dealing with preparation for leaving. The design of GOALS allows foster parents to structure, provide assistance, and plan the timing of activities according to their assessment of each child's needs.

Preparing Youth for Interdependent Living – Pasztor and Associates (1988) – Child Welfare Institute
This is a comprehensive curriculum developed by the Child Welfare Institute, in collaboration with the Center for the Study of Child Welfare at the University of Connecticut School of Social Work. The curriculum seeks to place the issues around preparation for inter-dependence within a framework of the developmental needs of adolescents and the processes of permanency planning. It emphasizes the central role of foster parents and provides them with some of the necessary supports to work effectively as partners in helping youth in foster care move into interdependent living.

Among its basic premises are:

1 Most adults have a network of family, friends, employment and community resources with which they live 'interdependently'. Foster care youth, as well, must be prepared for interdependent living.
2 In addition to helping young people develop tangible skills in daily living, interdependent living requires the formation of a positive self-concept and identity necessary for leading a satisfying, product-ive life.
3 In order to plan for the future, young people need help to make sense of their past. Every effort must be made to involve the birth family in interdependent living preparation.
4 Foster parents and foster care workers, as a team, can provide the most significant resources in preparing youth for interdependent living.

The curriculum includes the following specific topics:
– Partnership role of foster parents, foster care workers, and the community in preparing foster youth for interdependent living

- Understanding the special developmental needs of youth in foster care
- Assessing interdependent living strengths and needs
- Making connections: helping a youth to understand his or her past in order to plan for the future
- Making connections: helping a youth to rebuild and maintain ties with birth and extended families
- Developing life management skills
- Finding and using community resources
- Leaving foster care and other post emancipation issues.

The curriculum makes use of a variety of adult education approaches, including an audio taped demonstration of an independent living assessment tool and a videotape on major themes involved in preparing youth for adult life.

Training on child sexual abuse

Various agencies in the UK and the US are offering training for foster parents on child sexual abuse, in response to the growing number of young people coming into care with a history of abuse. An example from the UK follows:

Child Sexual Abuse – Training Programme for Foster Parents with Teenage Placements – Davis, Kidd and Pringle (1987) – Barnardo's
This manual was developed from a training project developed by Barnardo's north-east division for their family placement project. The aim of the paper is to assist foster parents to help young people who have been sexually abused. The foster parents who are part of the family placement project are regarded as professional and are given initial and ongoing help throughout the placements. This paper is not intended to be a complete training course on child sexual abuse. Its role is to assist foster parents to ask the 'right questions', not merely of the issues but, more importantly, of themselves. Chapter 1 describes the reasons for undertaking the programme and its objectives. Chapter 2 outlines the process by which the programme was devised. In Chapter 3, there is provided a resumé of the programme's content. Chapter 4 reviews the response of the foster parents to the programme and lessons learnt for the future. The training manual lists references and provides several appendices including a 'handbook' which was given to the project families and which encompasses in detail the content of the information sessions. Appendices also include exercises

used in some of the sessions and a questionnaire to evaluate foster parents' responses.

TRAINING FOSTER PARENTS – ISSUES AND GUIDELINES

The training curricula discussed in the preceding sections stress the importance of collaboration and partnership-building between foster parents and social workers. Learning activities that contribute to the growth and nurturing of partnership are crucial if the needs of youth moving out of care are to be met.

What remains somewhat unclear among child welfare professionals is whether preparation for interdependent living is a primary care-giving responsibility or one that involves a more specialized role for foster parents. This mirrors the field's current ambivalence as to whether it is the responsibility of child welfare agencies to prepare *all* adolescents in foster care for the task of young adulthood as part of its core services, or instead, reserve that work only for those adolescents whose actual discharge plan indicates independent living as the placement goal.

This issue has major implications for youth in care. If the preparatory work is to begin only after the preferred options of family reunification or adoption are entirely eliminated from the plan for the adolescent, it is likely that, for many adolescents, the preparatory process will begin quite late in their placement with the agency, leaving little time for intervention. This will also mean that the planning of work will occur on the agency's time clock rather than on the youngster's 'developmental clock'. (See Chapter 6 for further discussion of this issue.)

It is our strongest view that the service plan for *all* adolescents in foster care should include components designed to help them develop the skills and social and emotional supports that will promote more successful interdependent living, irrespective of the planned outcome. This would permit more planned proactive rather than reactive work with the adolescents as well as respecting their developmental needs. Agency policies and standards for care have not yet addressed these issues and it is apparent that, as these questions are resolved, foster parent training will more clearly reflect the fit of this work with foster parents' overall roles and responsibilities.

Assessing agency readiness for foster parent training

At the individual agency level, foster parent training must also be placed

159

in context and viewed as one component in the agency's overall foster care program. This section focuses on the emerging and recurring issues to be attended to in the planning and delivery of foster parent training within the organization's system of foster care services for adolescents.

The essential role of the trainer is providing an educational experience that meets program goals; and the learning needs of the participants cannot be overstated. Both in the US and the UK, most trainers in foster parent education represent a range of child welfare practitioners who have experience with, and interest in, working with foster parents. Public and private agency caseworkers, supervisors, and administrators, experienced foster parents, and staff from counselling and academic centers are likely instructors. In designing training programs for a specific agency, trainers might like to consider the following points, which will be examined below:

   i The relationship of foster parent training in general to the agency's foster care program;
   ii The agency's program for preparing youth for interdependent living;
   iii Agency assumptions about foster parents' roles;
   iv The trainer's knowledge of skill building areas;
   v The trainer's preparation and readiness to deliver training.

i The relationship of foster parent training in general to the agency's foster care program An organization's foster parent training program will become more effective in meeting participants' learning needs, as well as fitting with the overall foster care program, if organizational behavior reflects that:

1 The agency has clearly defined the purpose and goals of its foster parent training program.
2 The agency has clearly communicated this information to staff and foster parents.
3 Foster parent training is seen as an essential component in the agency's delivery of services and is not thought of as something 'extra'.
4 Foster parents and direct line staff have been involved in determining training needs.
5 There is administrative support to implement the training, and adequate resources allocated to support its development.

ii The agency's program for preparing youth for interdependent living The issues and strategies discussed in training need to be consonant with the stage of development in the agency's program for successfully preparing youth in foster care for interdependent living. An honest look by agency employees at their own practice and a desire to grow professionally to meet changing needs is required as a starting point. Training efforts will be enhanced if the agency has considered the following guidelines:

1 The agency has clearly defined its own policy and role in preparing youth in foster care for interdependent living.
2 The agency has communicated this information to staff and parents.
3 Preparation for interdependent living is viewed as an integral part of service planning for adolescents in care.
4 Workers and foster parents are able to discuss their individual and complementary roles in preparing youth for interdependent living.
5 The goals of training foster parents and workers to prepare youth for interdependent living have been determined.
6 The training is geared for both foster parents and workers.
7 The agency understands the significance of building community based resource networks.

iii Agency assumptions about foster parents' roles Trainers will have general assumptions about foster parents' roles. It is important that they check out organizational behavior to make sure that it is consistent with these assumptions. If it is not, the first task is to establish a baseline of the agency's expectation about foster parents. Training should begin with the following mutually agreed principles:

1 Foster parents' work with children involves physical care, emotional support, and parenting skills that help the child move on to the next stage of developmental progress.
2 Foster parents are expected to play an essential role in meeting the child's permanency planning needs.
3 Foster parents are viewed and treated as members of the agency's service delivery team.
4 Partnership building between social worker and foster parent actually occurs.
5 A network of supportive services is available to foster families.
6 Foster parenting children with 'special needs' requires the development of more specialized skills.

In addition, various principles pertain specifically to foster parents' roles in preparing youth for interdependent living. A useful starting point for trainers is to assess the extent to which their agency is moving in the following directions:

1 Foster parents' strengths in teaching interdependent living skills through daily living experiences are recognized and valued.
2 Foster parents have a designated role in helping assess the youth's preparatory needs.
3 Foster parents and workers are in partnership in addressing the interdependent living needs of the youth.
4 Foster parents and workers strive to engage the youth as a member of the partnership, recognizing that the youth's active involvement is crucial.
5 Foster parents are encouraged to provide the youth with:
   – experiential learning experiences that promote skill development;
   – experiences that show success and increase self-esteem;
   – opportunities to make decisions;
   – opportunities to make mistakes and still be supported;
   – opportunities to develop relationships outside the family.
6 The agency has addressed the problem of support and technical assistance required by foster parents.

iv Trainer's knowledge of skill building areas A comprehensive foster parent training program related to enhancing parents' skills in preparing youth for interdependent living requires a curriculum that will address the salient skill-building areas. The following list serves as an outline of principles that trainers might consider adopting:

1 Foster parents' skills in teaching youth tangible life management skills (such as cooking, health care, shopping, budgeting) are enhanced.
2 Foster parents' skills in teaching the more 'intangible' skills (such as decision-making, problem-solving, managing anger, dealing with loss, interpersonal relationships development) are enhanced.
3 Partnership building activities and conflict resolution experiences between foster parents and social workers are created.
4 Supporting the developmental needs of youth in foster care, especially those related to self-esteem and identity, is stressed and recognized as essential to successful transition out of care.
5 Foster parents learn how to engage young people in discussion of their own needs and goals.
6 Foster parents understand the importance of helping youth make sense of prior life experiences.

7 Foster parents learn skills to help youth rebuild or maintain ties with their own family members.

8 Foster parents learn strategies for involving youth with the community in a constructive manner.

9 Foster parents learn skills to successfully manage the separation process.

10 Foster parents have ample opportunities to share their expertise with one another.

These principles are also relevant to training for social work staff. Although training may be delivered to foster parents alone, joint training approaches for foster parents and workers are especially effective in supporting their complementary roles and needs, and are more likely to meet the needs of youth in care.

v Trainers' preparation and readiness to deliver training There is a wide array of issues that a trainer might consider in preparing to deliver foster parent training. Certainly the issues already discussed bear relationship to the trainer's capacity to make the foster parent training program a rich experience for the participants and a valuable component to the agency's overall foster care program. The following statements may be used by the trainer as a 'checklist' to explore his or her personal readiness for delivering training. They help identify strengths and give direction with regard to learning and support that may be needed by the trainer.

As I prepare for training with foster parents and staff, I . . .

– am aware of the challenging tasks created for foster parents in caring for adolescents.

– recognize the turmoil that may be created for foster families in parenting adolescents.

– understand the unique developmental needs of adolescents in foster care.

– understand the effects of the youth's previous life experiences on his/her present personality, behavior, and needs.

– recognize the adolescent's potential for continued growth and development.

– value the contribution foster parents make in parenting adolescents in care.

– recognize that a team approach that also engages the youth in partnership is critical to effective work with adolescents.

- understand that behavior management and discipline issues are major concerns to foster parents.
- realize that adolescents need opportunities to become increasingly responsible and more self-sufficient.
- can communicate my understanding of these issues and integrate them into the training program.
- agree with the purpose of the training course or program.
- understand its design and format.
- possess adequate knowledge and content 'competency' to deliver the training.
- recognize the differential nature of foster parent training compared with other adult learning programs.
- understand the essentials of adult education principles and possess the groupwork skills that will create opportunities for active learning, empowerment, and mutual support.
- can use a variety of teaching methods and 'tricks of the trade' to meet course goals and participants' needs.
- am aware of my own values regarding foster parents and children in care.
- have sufficient preparation time available to me.
- have developed strategies for ongoing evaluation of the training.
- can ask for technical assistance from the agency.
- have adequate 'comfort' resources (room, supplies, snacks, etc.).

If co-training:

- there has been time to become comfortable with my co-leader;
- division of labor has been discussed;
- our co-leader conflict issues can be raised and resolved.

This section has presented key issues and themes involved in preparing and delivering a successful foster parent training program within a detailed framework. A next step for trainers would be the development of an agency workplan in which goals and activities aimed at enhancing the system are outlined and implemented. The result of such a process would be more honest dialogue, more comprehensive and integrated training and programming, more skilled foster parents and staff and, most importantly, an enhanced system for meeting the needs of youth in foster care.

CONCLUSION

Foster parent training reflects the constantly evolving roles of foster parents, which parallel changes and advances in foster care practice. Assisting foster parents to fulfill effective roles in helping youth to prepare for interdependent living will require broad systematic changes. Adequate training, while a key support, is one of many interrelated factors. Other supports are needed.

Ironically, as the system becomes more complex and the needs of the children in care greater, the resources have become fewer. Fairly or not, we have placed a higher expectation for success on foster parents even while we know that adolescents, especially those in foster care, are a challenge to work with. Furthermore, parenting in general in these times is difficult, at best; and the other components of the care system, especially resources, have not kept pace with new demands. Hence, there are wide gaps between the reality and our ideal of service for young people in foster care. While training for foster parents will inevitably be viewed in light of these realities, it must also strive for the ideal so that young people exiting from the care system may enter society as adult citizens with at least the same life chances as their non-care peers.

Glossary of UK and US terms

We have divided this Glossary into two parts: first an elaboration of terms used in the United Kingdom, which may be unfamiliar to American readers and, second, an elaboration of those terms used in the United States which may be unfamiliar to British readers.

UK usage	*US equivalent*
Barnardo's	A leading British voluntary child welfare agency
Boarding out	The practice of using foster homes for children and youth
Boarding out regulations	Government regulations which define the use of foster family care, including the number of visits to be made by social workers and the issues to be taken into account when selecting foster families
Care proceedings	A legal process leading to a court hearing generally promoted by a public welfare agency to seek the transfer of parental rights to that agency
Care order	This is the order made as a result of care proceedings. It is a compulsory order which may last until a young person is 18
Child care	Child welfare
Curtis Report 1946	A major government White Paper (see below) upon which major pieces of child welfare legislation still used today was based

Dartington	A major research unit in Devon, England, which specializes in child welfare research
Department of Health and Social Security	A central government department which is responsible for providing social welfare and health programs. It is also concerned with income support (social security) and the provision of social work services as well as being responsible for the National Health Service
English local government board	The organization under the Poor Laws in the nineteenth century which was responsible for the care of the poor and homeless
Fostering	The practice of using family foster care
Foster care	Foster family care, not residential group care or group homes
Fostering officer	A specialist caseworker who may both select and supervise foster homes and undertake social work intervention with children's families and their foster parents
In care/local authority care	A legal provision whereby a local government social services department can assume responsibility for children and young people under the age of 18 who have serious personal or family problems
Leaving care	Emancipating from care
Local Authority/Social Services Department	A department of local government which provides social work services for individuals within a community. It embraces many client groups – children, families, elderly people with a range of difficulties, and adults and children who are disabled, mentally ill, physically or mentally handicapped

Rehabilitation | Reunification

Scheme | A program or project e.g. training demonstration, research, innovative practice

Specialist fostering | Giving an emphasis to a particular branch of foster care. This could be for a specialized purpose, e.g. assessment, treatment or the preparation for emancipation from care. It could also refer to foster family care for specific client groups such as adolescents with difficulties or children with handicaps

Termination of parental rights | A legal process, sometimes through a court, to transfer legal rights to a public welfare agency which has been providing foster or residential child care over a specified period of time

Welfare principle | Section 18(1) of the Child Care Act 1980. 'In reaching any decision relating to a child in their care, a local authority shall give first consideration to the need to safeguard and promote the welfare of the child throughout his childhood; and shall so far as practicable ascertain the wishes and feelings of the child regarding the decision and give due consideration to them, having regard to his age and understanding.'

White Paper | A government document, preceding a formal bill, which outlines proposals for changes in the law in any field

US usage | *UK usage*

Emancipation | Leaving care

Foster care	Care in a foster family mainly; sometimes used to denote any type of 'out-of-home' placement such as residential care for children
Job Training and Partnership Act	National legislation focusing on training young people for employment, in collaboration with community agencies and employers
Private/volunteer agency	Charitable organization in the personal social services and other fields
Protective services	Social services for abused and neglected children and their families
Public agency	Local, county or state government agency providing one or more types of social services e.g. a public child welfare agency
Public Law 96–272	National Law enacted in 1980 – The Adoption Assistance and Child Welfare Act – which focuses on reshaping public care provided by the states, through a variety of procedural reforms, fiscal incentives and permanency planning services for children in care or at risk of entering care
Reunification	Rehabilitation
Social Services Department	The unit of governmental or charitable agency, hospital or other organization which provides social services such as child care
US Department of Health and Human Services	National governmental agency with overall responsibility for coordination, administration and monitoring of the implementation by the states of national policies in the areas of health and mental health, income maintenance, child care and substance abuse

Appendix: Addresses of Agencies and Organizations Referred to in the Book

Barnardo's,
Tanners Lane,
Barkingside,
Ilford,
Essex IG6 1QG

British Agencies for Adoption and
Fostering,
11 Southwark Street,
Southwark
London SE1 1RQ

Black and in Care,
20 Compton Terrace,
London N1 2UN

Cherwell Housing Association,
209, Iffley Road,
Oxford

Dartington Research Unit,
The Courtyard,
Dartington Hall,
Totnes,
Devon TQ9 6EJ

First Key,
Hartley House,
Green Walk,
London SE1 4TV

Family Rights Group,
6–9 Manor Gardens,
Holloway Road,
London N7 6LA

National Foster Care Association,
Francis House,
Francis Street,
London SW1P 1DE

National Society for the Prevention
of Cruelty to Children,
67 Saffron Hill,
London EC1N 8RS

National Association of Young
People in Care,
20 Compton Terrace,
London N1 2UN

Parents' Aid,
66 Chippingfield,
Harlow,
Essex CM17 6DJ

RAFT (Rented Accommodation for
Teenagers),
Wincheap Centre,
37 Wincheap,
Canterbury,
Kent CT1 3RX

The Voice of the Child in Care,
60, Carysfort Road,
Hornsey,
London N8

US AGENCIES AND ORGANIZATIONS

Child Welfare League of America,
440 First Street, N.W.
Washington, D.C. 20001

Center for the Study of Child Welfare,
The University of Connecticut,
School of Social Work,
1798 Asylum Avenue,
West Hartford,
Connecticut 06117

Eastern Michigan University,
Institute for the Study of Children and
Families,
Ypsilanti,
Michigan 48197

Nova University,
1776 North Pine Island Road,
Suite 200
Plantation,
Florida 33322

New York State Child Welfare
Training Institute,
State University College at Buffalo,
1300 Elmwood Avenue,
Bacon Hall, 117,
Buffalo,
New York 14222

Orphan Foundation,
1500 Massachusetts Avenue, N.W.
Suite 448,
Washington, D.C. 20044

CANADIAN AGENCIES AND ORGANIZATIONS

Youth Horizons Center,
6 Weredale Park,
Westmount, Quebec,
Canada, H3Z 1Y6

Villa Marie Social Service Center,
4515 Saint Catherine St., West,
Montreal,
Canada

Children's Home Society of
Winnipeg,
400–777 Portage Avenue,
Winnipeg,
Manitoba,
Canada

References

AHMED, S., 'Blinkered by Background', *Community Care*, 13 Oct. 1983, pp. 20–22.

AHMED, S., CHEETHAM, J. and SMALL, J. (eds) *Social Work with Black Children and their Families*, London, Batsford, 1986.

ALDGATE, J., *Identification of Factors Influencing Children's Length of Stay in Care*, unpublished Ph.D. thesis, University of Edinburgh, 1977.

ALDGATE, J., 'Identification of Factors Influencing Children's Length of Stay in Care', in Triseliotis, J. (ed) *New Developments in Foster Care and Adoption*, London and Boston, Routledge and Kegan Paul, 1980, pp. 22–40.

ALDGATE, J., 'Work with Children Experiencing Separation and Loss: a Theoretical Framework', in Aldgate, J. and Simmonds, J. (eds) *Direct Work with Children*, London, Batsford, 1988, pp. 36–48.

ALDGATE, J. and HAWLEY, D., *Recollections of Disruption – A Study of Foster Care Breakdown*, London, National Foster Care Association, 1986.

ALDGATE, J. and SIMMONDS, J. (eds) *Direct Work with Children*, London, Batsford, 1988.

ALDGATE, J., COLTON, M. and HEATH, A. F., 'The Educational Attainment of Children in Care', *Adoption and Fostering*, vol. 11, no. 1, 1987, pp. 3–4.

ALTORFER, J., and O'DONNELL, B., *Report of Independent Living Subsidy Program Review*, Salem, OR., Oregon Children's Services Division, 1978.

ANSELL, D., *Making It On Your Own*, Richmond, VA., Region III Resource Center for Children, Youth and Families, School of Social Work, Viginia Commonwealth University, 1983.

ARMOR, D., POLICK, M. and STAMBUL, H., *Alcoholism and Treatment*, Santa Monica, California, The Rand Corporation, 1976.

ASSOCIATION OF BRITISH ADOPTION AND FOSTERING AGENCIES, *Report of the Steering Group of the Soul Kids Campaign*, London, Association of British Adoption and Fostering Agencies, 1977.

AUST, P., 'Using the Life Story Books in Treatment of Children in Placement', *Child Welfare*, vol. 60, no. 8, 1981, pp. 553–60.

BARNARDO'S NEW FAMILIES PROJECT, *Bridge Families Scheme*, Colchester, Barnardo's New Families Project, 1983.

BARNARDO'S NEW FAMILIES PROJECT, *Compass Information for Young People*, Colchester, Barnardo's New Families Project, 1988.

BARTH, R. P., 'Social Support Networks in Services for Adolescents and Their Families', in Whittaker, J. K., Garbarino, J. and associates, *Social Support Networks: Informal Helping in the Human Services*, New York, Aldine Publishing Co., 1983, pp. 299–331.

BARTH, R. P. *Social and Cognitive Treatment of Children and Adolescents*, San Francisco, CA., Jossey-Bass Publishing, 1986.

BARTH, R. P., and BERRY, M., 'Outcomes of Child Welfare Services under Permanency Planning', *Social Service Review*, vol. 61, no. 1, 1987, pp. 71–90.

BARTH, R. P. and BERRY, M., *Older Child Adoption and Disruption: Rates, Risks and Responses*, Hawthorne, NY., Aldine de Gruyter, 1988.

BAYLESS, L., *Road to Independent Living: A Guide Book for the Teenager*, Fort Lauderdale, FLA., Nova University, 1986.

BENNETT, T., Guide for Families with Children in Care, 4th. edn, Harlow, Parents' Aid, 1987.

BERKOWITZ, I. H., 'Value of Group Counseling in Secondary Schools', in Feinstein, S. C. (eds) *Adolescent Psychiatry, Developmental and Clinical Studies*, no. 14, Chicago, University of Chicago Press, 1987, pp. 522–45.

BERRIDGE, D. and CLEAVER, H., *Foster Home Breakdown*, Oxford, Basil Blackwell, 1987.

BEYER, M., 'Overcoming Emotional Obstacles to Independence', *Children Today*, vol. 15, 1986, pp. 8–12.

BLICK, L. C. and PORTER, F. S., 'Group Therapy with Female Adolescent Incest Victims', in Sgroi, S. M. (ed) *Handbook of Clinical Intervention in Child Sexual Abuse*, Lexington, Mass., Lexington Books, 1982, pp. 147–75.

BLOCK, N. M. and LIBOWITZ, A. S., *Recidivism in Foster Care*, New York, Child Welfare League of America, 1983.

BLUMENTHAL, K., and WEINBERG, A. (eds) *Establishing Parent Involvement in Foster Care Agencies*, New York, Child Welfare League of America, 1984.

BOATMAN, B., BORKAN, E. L. and SCHETKY, D. H., 'Treatment of Child Victims of Incest', *American Journal of Family Therapy*, vol. 9, no. 4, 1981, pp. 43–51.

BORKMAN, R., 'The Influence of Family Visiting upon Boys' Behavior in a Juvenile Correctional Institution', *Child Welfare*, vol. 66, no. 6, 1985, pp. 629–38.

BORKMAN, R., 'Problems of Sexually Abused Girls and Their Treatment', *Social Casework*, vol. 65, no. 3, 1984, pp. 182–6.

BOWLBY, J., Attachment and Loss, vol. 1: Attachment, London, Hogarth Press, 1969.

BOWLBY, J., *The Making and Breaking of Affectional Bonds*, London, Tavistock, 1977.

BRADY, J., 'Advantages and Problems of Using Written Contracts', *Social Work*, vol. 27, 1982, pp. 275–7.

BREAKWELL, G. M., *Threatened Identities*, Chichester, Wiley, 1983.

BREAKWELL, G. M., *Coping with Threatened Identities*, London, Methuen, 1986.

BRIM, O. and KAGAN, J. (eds) *Constancy and Change in Human Development*, Harvard, Harvard University Press, 1980.

BRIN, M., PILOWY, M., WALLACE, W., WASSON, D. and WOLF, M., *Training Foster Parents of Adolescents*, Buffalo, NY., New York State Child Welfare Training Institute, State University College at Buffalo, 1985.

BRINDIS, C., BARTH, R. P. and LOOMIS, A., 'Continuous Counseling: Case Management with Teenage Parents', *Social Casework*, vol. 68, 1987, pp. 164–72.

BRONFENBRENNER, U., *The Ecology of Human Developments*, Cambridge, Mass., Harvard University Press, 1979.

BROOKS, J., *The Process of Parenting*, Paolo Alto, California, Mayfield, 1981.

BRUMMER, N., 'White Social Workers, Black Children', in Aldgate, J. and Simmonds, J. (eds), 1988, op. cit., pp. 75–86.

BRYANT, B., 'Special Foster Care: a History and Rationale', *Journal of Clinical Child Psychology*, vol. 10, no. 1, 1981, pp. 8–20.

BURCH, M., 'Shared Care and Shared Responsibilities – a Foster Parent's View', in Family Rights Group (ed) *Promoting Links: Keeping Children and Families in Touch*, London, Family Rights Group, 1986, pp. 114–19.

BUSH, M. and GORDON, A. C., 'The Case for Involving Children in Child Welfare Decisions', *Social Work*, vol. 27, no. 4, 1982, pp. 309–14.

BUSH, M., GORDON, A. C. and LeBAILLY, R., 'Evaluating Child Welfare Services: a Contribution from the Clients'. *Social Service Review*, vol. 51, no. 3, 1977, pp. 491–501.

CAUTLEY, P. W. *New Foster Parents – The First Experience*, New York, Human Sciences Press, 1980.

CHESTNUT, M., *A Survey on Emancipation Beliefs and Practices of Social Providers*, unpublished manuscript, University of California, Berkeley, School of Social Welfare, 1985.

CLARKSON, A. and WISTLECRAFT, R., 'Foster Parent Training in Coventry', *Adoption and Fostering*, vol. 11, no. 3, 1987, pp. 31–5.

CHILD WELFARE LEAGUE OF AMERICA, *Parenting Plus*, New York, Child Welfare League of America, 1975.

CHILD WELFARE LEAGUE OF AMERICA, *Fostering Parenting in Adolescent*, New York, Child Welfare League of America, 1977 and 1985. (See also National Foster Care Association).

COOK, R., and ANSELL, D., *Independent Living Services for Youth in Foster Care*, Rockville, MD., Westat, Inc., 1986.

CORDELL, A. S., NATHAN, C. and Krymow, V. P., 'Group Counseling for Children Adopted at Older Ages', *Child Welfare*, vol. 64, no. 2, 1985, pp. 113–24.

CORDEN, J. J. and PRESTON-SHOOT, M., *Contracts in Social Work*, Aldershot, England and Brookfield, VT., Gower, 1987.

CRONBACH, L. J. and GLESER, G. C., *Psychological Tests and Personnel Decisions*, Urbana, Illinois, University of Illinois Press, 2nd edn, 1967.

CURTIS REPORT, *Report of the Care of Children Committee*, Cmnd. 6922, London, Her Majesty's Stationary Office, 1946.

DAVIS, E., KIDD, L. and PRINGLE, K., *Child Sexual Abuse: Training Programme for Foster Parents with Teenage Placements*, Newcastle-upon Tyne, Barnardo's, 1987.

DAVIS, I. P., *Adolescents – Theoretical and Helping Perspectives*, Hingham, Mass., Kluwer-Nijhoff Publishing, 1985.

DAVIS, L. J. and BLAND, D. C., 'The Use of Foster Parents as Role Models for Parents', in Sinanaglu, P. A. and Malluccio, A. N. (eds) *Parents of Children in Placement: Perspectives and Programs*, New York, Child Welfare League of America, 1981, pp. 415–21.

DAVIS, S., MORRIS, B. and THORN, J., 'Task-centred Assessment for Foster Parents', *Adoption and Fostering*, vol. 8, no. 4, 1984, pp. 33–7.

DEPARTMENT OF HEALTH AND SOCIAL SECURITY, Social Work Service, *A Study of the Boarding Out of Children*, London, Her Majesty's Stationery Office, 1981.

DEPARTMENT OF HEALTH AND SOCIAL SECURITY, *Code of Practice: Access to Children in Care*, London, Her Majesty's Stationery Office, 1983.

DEPARTMENT OF HEALTH AND SOCIAL SECURITY, *Social Work Decisions in Child Care*, London, Her Majesty's Stationery Office, 1985.

DEPARTMENT OF HEALTH AND SOCIAL SECURITY, *Children in Care in England And Wales*, London, Her Majesty's Stationery Office, 1986.

DORCUS, R. M. and JAMES, M. L., *Handbook of Personnel Selection*, New York, McGraw Hill, 1950.

DOLAN, D. and O'NEILL, L., 'Helping the Foster Child at College and at Preparatory School', *New York Times*, 13 November 1983, p. 15.

DUBOIS, D., MOCKLER, B., and G., 'Foster Parents as Key Workers', *Adoption and Fostering*, vol. 8, no. 3, 1984, pp. 30–1.

DVORAK, J. T. and MASON, J. L., *Ready or not . . . Emancipation Planning for Youth in Substitute Care: A Workbook*, Portland, OR., Regional Research Institute for Human Services, 1985.

EASTMAN, K., 'The Foster Family in a Systems Perspective', *Child Welfare*, vol. 58, no. 9, 1979, pp. 564–70.

ERIKSON, E., *Identity: Youth and Crisis*, London, Faber and Faber, 1968.

EUSTER, S. D. and NOBLE, L. S., 'A Unique Approach to Foster Parent Training: Preliminary Caseworkers as Instructors', *Journal of Continuing Social Work Education*, vol. 1, 1981, pp. 7–10, 32, 34.

EUSTER, S. D., WARD, V. P., VARNER, J. G. and EUSTER, G. L., 'Life Skills Groups for Adolescent Foster Children', *Child Welfare*, vol. 63, no. 1, 1984, pp. 27–36.

FAHLBERG, V., *Helping Children When They Must Move*, London, British Agencies for Adoption and Fostering, 1981.

FAMILY RIGHTS GROUP (ed.) *Promoting Links: Keeping Children and Families in Touch*, London, Family Rights Group, 1986.

175

FANSHEL, D., 'Parental Visiting of Children in Foster Care: Key to Discharge?', *Social Service Review*, vol. 49, no. 4, 1975, pp. 493–514.

FANSHEL, D. *On the Road to Permanency: An Expanded Data Base for Service to Children in Foster Care*, New York, Child Welfare League of America, 1982.

FANSHEL, D. and GRUNDY, J., *CSIS/CCRS Special Report Series, New York State Reports*, New York, Columbia University, 1980.

FEIN, E., MALUCCIO, A., HAMILTON, V. J. and WARD, D. E. 'After Foster Care: Outcomes of Permanency Planning for Children', *Child Welfare*, vol. 62, no. 6, November/December 1983, pp. 485–562.

FESTINGER, T., *No One Ever Asked Us . . . A Postscript to Foster Care*, New York, Columbia University Press, 1983.

FINKELHOR, D. and BROWNE, A., 'Initial and Long-Term Effects: A Conceptual Framework', in Finkelhor, D. *et al.*, A Sourcebook on Child Sexual Abuse, Beverley Hills, California, Sage Publishing, 1985, pp. 180–98.

FOWLER, C., BURNS, S. R. and ROEHL, J. E., 'The Role of Group Therapy in Incest Counseling', *International Journal of Family Therapy*, vol. 5, no. 2, 1983, pp. 127–35.

FURRH, P. E., Jnr., 'Emancipation: The Supervised Apartment Living Approach', *Child Welfare*, vol. 62, 1983, pp. 54–62.

GAMBRILL, E. D., *Casework: A Competency-Based Approach*, New York, Prentice Hall, 1983.

GAMBRILL, E. D. and STEIN, T. J., 'Working with Biological Parents: Important Procedural Ingredients', *Children and Youth Services Review*, vol. 7, 1985, pp. 173–89.

GARBARINO, J., *Children and Families in the Social Environment*, New York, Aldine Publishing Company, 1982.

GARBARINO, J., GUTTMAN, E. and SEELEY, J. W., *The Psychologically Battered Child*, San Francisco, Jossey-Bass Publishers, 1986.

GARBARINO, J., SCHELLENBACH, C. J., SEBES, J. M. and Associates, *Troubled Youth, Troubled Families: Understanding Families At-Risk for Adolescent Maltreatment*, New York, Aldine Publishing Co., 1986.

GEORGE, V., *Foster Care: Theory and Practice*, London, Routledge and Kegan Paul, 1970.

GEORGE, V., 'Origins and Development of the Boarding Out System', *Social Services News*, no. 2, October 1971 to April 1972, pp. 1–7.

GERMAIN, C. B. and GITTERMAN, A., *The Life Model of Social Work Practice*, New York, Columbia University Press, 1980.

GIBSON, P. and PARSLOE, P., 'What Stops Parental Access to Children In Care'?, *Adoption and Fostering*, vol. 8, no. 1, 1984, pp. 18–24.

GILDERSLEEVE, G., 'Skills in Working with Adolescents,' *Adoption and Fostering*, vol. 12, no. 1, 1988, pp. 23–5.

GODEK, S., *Leaving Care*, London, Barnardo's Social Work Papers, no. 2, 1976.

GOLDBERG, E. M., GIBBONS, J. and SINCLAIR, I., *Problems, Tasks and Outcomes*, London, Allen & Unwin, 1985.

GUERNEY, L. F., *Foster Parent Training: Adolescent Supplement*, State College, PA., Pennsylvania State University, 1978.

GUERNEY, L. F., 'Prospects for Intervention with Troubled Youth and Troubled Families' in Garbarino, J. and associates, 1986, op. cit., pp. 255–79.

HALM, D., *Independent Living Program Review*, Salem, OR., Oregon Children's Services Division, 1980.

HARTMAN, A., *Finding Families: An Ecological Approach to Finding Families in Adoption*, New York, Sage Human Services, 1979.

HARTMAN, A. and LAIRD, J., *Family-Centred Social Work Practice*, New York, Free Press, 1983.

HARTUP, W. W., 'Peer Relations', in *Mussen Handbook of Child Psychology*, 4th edn, vol. 4, 1984, pp. 122–96.

HAZEL, N., *A Bridge to Independence*, Oxford and New York, Basil Blackwell, 1981.

HAZEL, N., 'RAFT Review (Rented Accommodation for Teenagers)', unpublished report, 1988.

HERBERT, M., *Living with Teenagers*, Oxford and New York, Basil Blackwell, 1987.

HESS, P. M., 'Parental Visiting of Children in Foster Care: Current Knowledge and Research Agenda', *Children and Youth Services Review*, vol. 9, no. 1, 1987, pp. 29–50.

HOFMAN, P. J. and COLE, E. P., 'Bridging the Gap Between Youth and Community Services: A Life Skills Education Program', *Children Today*, vol. 12, 1983, pp. 17–22.

HOGHUGHI, M. S., *The Delinquent*, London, Burnett Books, Hutchinson, 1983.

HOGHUGHI, M. S., DOBSON, C., LYONS, J., MUCKLEY, A. and SWAINSTON, M., *Assessing Problem Children*, London, Burnett Books, André Deutsch, 1980.

HOGHUGHI, M. S., *Treating Problem Children*, London, Burnett Books, Hutchinson, 1985.

HOLMAN, R., 'New Ways to Select Foster Parents', *New Society*, 26.3.64.

HOREJSI, C. R., BERTSCHE, A. V. and CLARKE, F. W., *Social Work Practice with Parents in Foster Care: A Handbook*, Springfield, Illinois, Charles C. Thomas Pub, 1981.

HORNBY, H. C. and COLLINS, M. I., 'Teenagers in Foster Care: The Forgotten Majority', *Children and Youth Services Review*, vol. 3, 1981, pp. 7–20.

HORST, P., *Psychological Measurement and Prediction*, Belmont, CA., Wadsworth Publishing, 1966.

HUDSON, B. L. and MACDONALD, G. M., *Behavioural Social Work – An Introduction*, London, Macmillan, 1986.

HUTCHISON, E. D., 'Use of Authority in Direct Social Work Practice with Mandated Clients', *Social Services Review*, vol. 61, 1987, pp. 581–98.

JACKSON, S., *The Education of Children in Care*, Bristol, School of Applied Social Studies, University of Bristol, 1988.

JENKINS, S., 'The Tie that Bonds', in Malluccio, A. N. and Sinanoglu, P. A.

(eds) *The Challenge of Partnership: Working with Parents of Children in Foster Care*, New York, Child Welfare League of America, 1981, pp. 39–51.

JENKINS, S. and NORMAN, E., *Filial Deprivation and Foster Care*, New York, Columbia University Press, 1972.

JOHNSON, M. J. and NELSON, A., *Serving Adolescents in the Care of Child Welfare Agencies Through the Employment and Job Training Partnership Systems*, Boston, Judge Baker Guidance Center, 1986.

JOHNSTON E. and GABOR, P., 'Parent Counselors: a Foster Care Program with New Roles for Major Participants', in Maluccio, A. N. and Sinanoglu, P. A., eds., *The Challenge of Partnership: Working with Parents of Children in Foster Care*, New York, Child Welfare League of America, 1981, pp. 200–208.

JONES, M. A., *A Second Chance for Families – Five Years Later: Follow-up of a Program to Prevent Foster Care*, New York, Child Welfare League of America, 1983.

JONES, W., 'Alberta', *Adoption and Fostering*, no. 91, 1978, pp. 47–8.

JONES, M. A. and MOSES, B., *West Virginia's Former Foster Children: Their Experiences in Care and Their Lives as Young Adults*, New York, Child Welfare League of America, 1984.

JONES, R. and PRITCHARD, C. (eds) *Social Work with Adolescents*, London, Routledge and Kegan Paul, 1980.

KADUSHIN, A., 'Child Welfare', in Maas, H. S. (ed.) *Research in the Social Sciences: A Five Year Review*, New York, National Association of Social Workers, 1971, pp. 13–69.

KAGAN, R. M. and REID, W. J., 'Critical Factors in the Adoption of Emotionally Disturbed Youth', *Child Welfare*, vol. 65, no. 1, Jan/Feb 1986, pp. 63–73.

KAHAN, B., *Growing Up in Care*, Oxford, Basil Blackwell, 1979.

KATZ, L., 'Parental Stress and Factors for Success in Older-child Adoption', *Child Welfare*, vol. 65, no. 6, Nov/Dec 1986, pp. 569–78.

KAY, N., 'A Systematic Approach to Selecting Foster Parents', *Case Conference*, vol. 13, no. 2, 1966; reprinted in Tod, R. J. N. (ed.) *Social Work in Foster Care*, London, Longman, 1971, pp. 39–60.

KELLMER PRINGLE, M., *The Needs of Children*, London, Hutchinson, 1975. See also 3rd. edn, 1986.

KELLY, G., 'Access – The Research into Practice', in Family Rights Group (ed.) op. cit., 1986, pp. 20–32.

KLUGER, M., FEIN, E., MALUCCIO, A. and TAYLOR, J., *An Examination of Long-Term Foster Care*, Hartford, C. T., Child and Family Services, 1986.

LAIRD, J., 'An Ecological Approach to Child Welfare: Issues of Family Identity and Continuity', in Germain, C. B. (ed.) *Social Work Practice: People and Environments*, New York, Columbia University Press, 1979. pp. 174–209.

LAIRD, J. and HARTMAN, A. (eds) *A Handbook of Child Welfar – Context, Knowledge, and Practice*, New York, The Free Press, 1985.

LAKE, R., 'Adolescents and Parental Contact', *Adoption and Fostering*, vol. 11. no. 2, 1987, pp. 15–18.

LeCroy, C. W., 'Social Skills Training and Adolescents: A Review', *Child and Youth Services*, vol. 5, no. 3/4, 1982, pp. 91–116.

Lee, J. A. B., 'Group Work with Mentally Retarded Foster Adolescents', *Social Casework*, vol. 58, no. 3, 1977, pp. 164–73.

Lee, J. A. B., and Park, D. N., 'A Group Approach to the Depressed Adolescent Girl in Foster Care', *American Journal of Orthopsychiatry*, vol. 48, no. 3, 1978, pp. 516–27.

Lee, J. A. B. and Park, D. N., *Walk a Mile in my Shoes – A Manual on Biological Parents for Foster Parents*, W. Hartford, CT., Center for the Study of Child Welfare, University of Connecticut, 1980.

Levine, B., *Group Psychotherapy, Practice and Development*, Englewood Cliffs, NJ., Prentice-Hall Inc., 1979.

Lewis, K. G., 'Sibling Therapy with Children in Foster Homes', in Cambrinck-Graham, L. (ed.) *Treating Young Children in Family Therapy*, Rockville, MD., Aspen Publishers Inc., 1986, pp. 52–61.

Loppnow, D. M. 'Adolescents on Their Own', in Laird, J. and Hartmann, A., (eds.) 1983, op. cit., pp. 514–31.

Loppnow, D. M., *Fostering the Teenager*, Ypsilanti, MI., Institute for the Study of Children and Families, Eastern Michigan University, 1978.

Lupton, C., 'Preparation for Leaving Care', *Concern*, no. 57, Winter 1985–6, pp. 13–15.

McAdams, P. T., 'The Parent in the Shadows', in Sinanoglu, P. A. and Maluccio, A. N. (eds) *Parents of Children in Placement: Perspectives and Programs*, New York, Child Welfare League of America, 1981, pp. 307–12.

McDermott, V. A., 'Life Planning Services: Helping Older Placed Children with their Identity', *Child and Adolescent Social Work*, no. 4, 1987, pp. 97–115.

McFadden, E. J., 'Physical and Sexual Abuse of Adolescents in Foster Care', in Maluccio, A. N., Krieger, R. and Pine, B. (eds), in press, op. cit.

McGregor, D., *The Human Side of Enterprise*, New York, McGraw-Hill, 1960.

MacNeil, J., *Preparation of Independence: Planning and Learning for Independent Living*, unpublished manuscript, Ontario, Ministry of Community and Social Services, 1984.

MacVeigh, J., *Gaskin*, London, Jonathan Cape, 1982.

McWhinnie, A., 'Foster Parents' Study', in National Foster Care Association, *Foster Care, a Teamwork Service*, conference papers, First International Conference on Foster Care, Oxford, 1980, pp. 58–70.

Maas, H. S. and Engler, R. E., *Children in Need of Parents*, New York, Columbia University Press, 1959.

Maluccio, A. N., *Learning From Clients – Interpersonal Helping As Viewed by Clients and Social Workers*, New York, The Free Press, 1979.

Maluccio, A. N. (ed.) *Promoting Competence in Clients – A New/Old Approach to Social Work Practice*, New York, The Free Press, 1981.

Maluccio, A. N., 'Biological Families and Foster Care: Initiatives and Obstacles', in Cox, M. J. and Cox, R. D. (eds) *Foster Care: Current Issues,*

Policies and Practices, Norwood, NJ., Ablex Publishing Co-operation, 1985, pp. 147–66.

MALUCCIO, A. N. AND FEIN, E., 'Growing up in Foster Care', *Children and Youth Services Review*, vol. 7, no. 2/3, 1985, pp. 123–34.

MALUCCIO, A. N., FEIN, E. and OLMSTEAD, K. A., *Permanency Planning for Children – Concepts and Methods*, London and New York, Tavistock Publication and Methuen, 1986.

MALUCCIO, A. N., KRIEGER, R. and PINE, B., *Preparing Adolescents for Life After Foster Care: the Central Role of Foster Parents*, Washington, DC., Child Welfare League of America, in press.

MALUCCIO, A. N. and MARLOW, W. D., 'The Case for the Contract', *Social Work*, vol. 19, no. 1, Jan. 1974, pp. 28–36.

MALUCCIO, A. N. and SINANOGLU, P. A. (eds) *The Challenge of Partnership: Working with Parents of Children in Foster Care*, New York, Child Welfare League of America, 1981.

MANN, P., *Children in Care Revisited*, London, Batsford, 1984.

MAUZERALL, H. A., 'Emancipation from Foster Care: The Independent Living Project', *Child Welfare*, vol 62, 1983, pp. 46–53.

MAYER, J. and TIMMS, N., *The Client Speaks – Working-Class Impressions of Casework*, London and Boston, Routledge and Kegan Paul, 1970.

MILLHAM, S., BULLOCK, R., HOSIE, K. and HAAK, M., *Lost in Care*, London, Gower, 1986.

MONACO, M. and THOBURN, J., *Self-Help Groups for Parents with Children in Care*, Norwich, Social Work Monograph, University of East Anglia, 1987.

MOUZAKITIS, C. M., 'Characteristics of Abused Adolescents and Guidelines for Intervention', *Child Welfare*, vol. 63, no. 2, 1984, pp. 149–57.

MOUZAKITIS, C. M., and VARGHESE, R., 'Treatment of Child Neglect', in Mouzakitis, C. M. and Varghese, R. (eds) *Social Work Treatment with Abused and Neglected Children*, Springfield, Illinois, Charles C. Thomas, 1985, pp. 268–279.

NATIONAL ASSOCIATION OF YOUNG PEOPLE IN CARE, *Sharing Care*, Bradford, National Association of Young People in Care, 1983.

NATIONAL FOSTER CARE ASSOCIATION, *Introduction to Foster Parenting – Parenting Plus*, London, National Foster Care Association, 1980.

NATIONAL FOSTER CARE ASSOCIATION, *Added to Adolescence – Foster Parenting an Adolescent*, London, National Foster Care Association, 1982.

NATIONAL FOSTER CARE ASSOCIATION, *Towards A Discipline in Fostering*, London, National Foster Care Association, 1985.

NATIONAL FOSTER CARE ASSOCIATION, *About You and Fostering*, London, National Foster Care Association, 1987a.

NATIONAL FOSTER CARE ASSOCIATION, *Information Pack on Child Sexual Abuse*, London, National Foster Care Association, 1987b

NATIONAL FOSTER CARE ASSOCIATION, 'Foster Care Charter', *Foster Care*, no. 53, March, 1988, p. 40

ORPHAN FOUNDATION NEWSLETTER, 'Orphan Foundation Awards its First Scholarships', no. 3, Winter 1986, p. 1.

PACKMAN, J., *The Child's Generation*, 2nd edn, London, Basil Blackwell and Martin Robertson, 1981.

PACKMAN, J., *Who Needs Care? Social Work Decisions about Children*, Oxford and New York, Basil Blackwell, 1986.

PAGE, R. and CLARKE, G. (eds) *Who Needs Care?* London, National Children's Bureau, 1977.

PARKER, R. A., 'Foster Care in Context', *Adoption and Fostering*, vol. 93, no. 3, 1978, pp. 27–31.

PASZTOR, E. M., *Preparation for Fostering: Preservice Education for Families*, Fort Lauderdale, FLA., Nova University, 1983.

PASZTOR, E. M., *Model Approach to Partnerships in Parenting*, Atlanta, Georgia, Center for Foster and Residential Care, Child Welfare Institute, 1986.

PASZTOR, E. M., 'Permanency Planning and Foster Parenting: Implications for Recruitment, Selection, Training and Retention', *Children and Youth Services Review*, vol. 7, nos. 2, 3, 1985, pp. 191–205.

PASZTOR, E. M. and Associates, *Preparing Youth for Interdependent Living*, Atlanta, Georgia, Child Welfare Institute, 1988.

PASZTOR, E. M., CLARREN, J., TIMBERLAKE, E. M. and BAYLESS, K., 'Stepping Out of Foster Care into Independent Living', *Children Today*, vol. 15, 1986, pp. 32–5.

PILIAVIN, I., SOSIN, M. and WESTERFELT, H., 'Conditions Contributing to Long-Term Homelessness: An Exploratory Study', IRP discussion paper no. 853–887, Madison, WI., Institute for Research on Poverty, 1987.

PORTER, F. S., BLICK, L. C. and SGROI, S. M., 'Treatment of the Sexually Abused Child', in Sgroi, S. M. (ed.) *Handbook of Clinical Intervention in Child Sexual Abuse*, Lexington, Mass., Lexington Books, 1982, pp. 109–45.

PORTER, R., *Teenagers Leaving Care*, Norwich, Social Work Monograph, University of East Anglia, 1983.

PROCH, K. and TABER, M. A., 'Placement Disruption: A Review of Research', *Child and Youth Service Review*, vol. 7, 1985, pp. 309–20.

PROCH, K. and TABER, M. A., 'Alienated Adolescents in Foster Care', *Social Work Research and Abstracts*, vol. 23, no. 2, Summer 1987, pp. 9–13.

PUGH, G. and DE'ATH, E., *The Needs of Parents*, London, Macmillan, 1984.

PYM, D., 'The Misuse of Professional Manpower,' in Pym, D. (ed.) *Industrial Society: Social Sciences in Management*, London, Penguin Books, 1968.

QUINTON, D. and RUTTER, M., 'Parents with Children in Care: I. Current Circumstances and Parenting' and 'II. Intergenerational Continuities', *Journal of Child Psychology and Psychiatry*, vol. 25, no. 2, 1984, pp. 211–50.

RAUBOLT, R. R., 'Brief, Problem-Focused Group Psychotherapy with Adolescents', *American Journal of Orthopsychiatry*, vol. 53, no. 1, 1983, pp. 157–65.

REEVES, C., *Put It in Writing, A Study of Written Information Given to Parents of*

Children in Care, unpublished dissertation for MSc in Social Research, University of Surrey, 1986.

REST, E. R. and WATSON, K. W., 'Growing Up in Foster Care', *Child Welfare*, vol. 63, no. 4, 1984, pp. 291–306.

RICE, D. L. and MCFADDEN, E. J., 'A Forum for Foster Children, *Child Welfare*, vol. 68, no. 3, 1988, pp. 231–43.

ROBSON, P. 'First Key for Leaving Care', *Adoption and Fostering*, vol. 11, no. 2, 1987, pp. 19–21.

ROJEK, C. and COLLINS, S. A., 'Contract or Con Trick?', *British Journal of Social Work*, vol. 17, 1987, pp. 199–211.

ROSENBERG, S., 'Treatment of the Emotionally Disturbed, Mildly Retarded Youngster in the Foster Care System', *Child and Adolescent Social Work*, vol. 2, no. 1, 1985, pp. 49–59.

ROWE, J., *Fostering in the Eighties*, London, British Agencies for Adoption and Fostering, 1983a.

ROWE, J., 'Fostering Outcomes: Interpreting Breakdown Rates', *Adoption and Fostering*, vol. 11, no. 1, 1987, pp. 25, 32–4.

ROWE, J. and LAMBERT, L., *Children Who Wait*, London, Association of British Adoption Agencies, 1973.

ROWE, J., CAIN, H., HUNDLEBY, M. and KEANE, A., *Long-Term Foster Care*, London, Batsford, 1984.

ROWE, P., 'Bridging the Gap: From Foster Care to Independent Living', *Children Today*, vol. 12, 1983b, pp. 28–9.

RUSHTON, A. and TRESEDER, J., 'Research: Developmental Recovery', *Adoption and Fostering*, vol. 10, no. 3, 1986, pp. 54–6.

RUTTER, M. 'Resilience in the Face of Adversity', *British Journal of Psychiatry*, no. 147, 1985, pp. 598–611.

RYAN, P., *P-U-S-H for Youth G-O-A-L-S: Providing Understanding, Support and Help for Youth Going Out and Living Successfully*, Ypsilanti Michigan, Institute for the Study of Children and Families, Eastern Michigan University, 1987.

RYAN, P., MCFADDEN, E. J. and WARREN, B. L., 'Foster Families: A Resource for Helping Parents', in Maluccio, A. N. and Sinanoglu, P. A. (eds) 1981, op. cit., pp. 189–99.

RYAN, T. and WALKER, R., *Making Life Story Books*, British Agencies for Adoption and Fostering, 1985.

SALVATION ARMY, *Bridging the Gap Between Youth and Community Services – A Life Skills Education Progam: Leader's Guide*, New York, Salvation Army, 1982.

SCHAFFER, H. R. and EMERSON, P. E., 'The Development of Social Attachments in Infancy', *Monographs in Social Research and Child Development*, vol. 29, no. 3, 1964, p. 94.

SCHEIDLINGER, S., 'Group Treatment of Adolescents: An Overview', *American Journal of Orthopsychiatry*, vol. 55, no. 1, 1985, pp. 102–11.

SCHINKE, S. P. and GILCHRIST, L. D., *Life Skills Counseling with Adolescents*, Baltimore, University Park Press, 1984.

SCHOENFELD, P., 'Network Therapy: Clinical Theory and Practice with Disturbed Adolescents', *Psychotherapy*, vol. 21, no. 1, 1984, pp. 92–100.

SCURFIELD, R. M., 'Post-trauma Stress Assessment and Treatment: Overview and Formulations', in Figley, C. R. (ed) *Trauma and Its Wake*, New York, Brunner/Mazel Publishers, 1985, pp. 219–56.

SEABERG, J. R., 'Foster Parents as Aides to Parents', in Maluccio, A. N. and Sinanoglu, P. A. (eds) 1981, op. cit., pp. 209–20.

SEABURY, B. A., 'Negotiating Sound Contracts with Clients', *Public Welfare*, vol. 37, 1979, pp. 33–8.

SEABURY, B. A., 'The Beginning Phase: Engagement, Initial Assessment, and Contracting', in Laird, J. and Hartman, A., 1985, op. cit.

SEASHORE, M., *The Effectiveness of Foster Youth Services in Four California School Districts*, Report no. 1 of 1986, San Francisco, San Fransico State University Public Research Institute, 1986.

SELECT COMMITTEE ON CHILDREN, YOUTH AND FAMILES, *Fact Sheet*, Washington, D.C., U.S. House of Representatives, Sept. 1986.

SHAW, M., 'Substitute Parenting,' in Sluckin, W. and Herbert, M. (eds) *Parental Behaviour*, Oxford and New York, Basil Blackwell, 1986.

SHAW, M., *Family Placements for Children in Care – A Guide to the Literature*, London, British Agencies for Adoption and Fostering, 1988.

SHAW, M., and HIPGRAVE, T., *Specialist Fostering*, London, Batsford, 1983.

SIMONS, R. L. and MILLER, M. G., 'Adolescent Depression: Assessing the Impact of Negative Cognitions and Socioenvironmental Problems', *Social Work*, vol. 32, no. 4, 1987, pp. 326–30.

SINANOGLU, P. A. and MALUCCIO, A. N. (eds) *Parents of Children in Placement: Perspectives and Programs*, New York, Child Welfare League of America, 1981.

SLUCKIN, W. and HERBERT, M. (eds) *Parental Behaviour*, Oxford and New York, Basil Blackwell, 1986.

SMALL, J., 'Transracial Placements: Conflicts and Contradictions', in Ahmed, S., Cheetham, J. and Small, J. (eds) 1986, op. cit., pp. 81–99.

SMITH, C. R., *Adoption and Fostering: Why and How?*, London, Macmillan, 1984.

SNODGRASS, R. and BRYANT, B., 'Special Foster Care and Foster Family-Based Treatment Today: A National Survey of Current Programs', in Hawkins, R. P. and Breiling, J. (eds) *Therapeutic Foster Care: Critical Issues*, Washington, D.C., Child Welfare League of America, in press.

SPECHT, H., 'Social Support, Social Networks, Social Exchange and Social Work Practice', *Social Service Review*, vol. 60, no. 2, 1986, pp. 218–40.

SPECK, J. L. and SPECK, R. V., 'Social Network Intervention with Adolescents', in Mirkin, M. P. and Koman, S. L. (eds) *Handbook of Adolescents and Family Therapy*, New York, Gardner Press Inc., 1985, pp. 149–60.

STACEY, M., DEARDEN, R., PIL, R. and ROBINSON, D., *Hospitals, Children and Their Families: The Report of a Pilot Study*, London, Routledge and Kegan Paul, 1970.

STEIN, M. and CAREY, K., *Leaving Care*, Oxford and New York, Basil Blackwell, 1986.

STEIN, M. and ELLIS, S., *Gizza Say?*, Bradford, National Association of Young People in Care, 1976.

STEIN, M. D. and DAVIS, J. K., *Therapies for Adolescents*, San Francisco, Jossey-Bass Publishers, 1982.

STEIN, T. J., GAMBRILL, E. D. and WILTSE, K. T., *Children in Foster Homes – Achieving Continuity of Care*, New York, Praeger, 1978.

STEIN, T. J. and RZEPNICKI, T., *Decision Making at Child Welfare Intake*, New York, Child Welfare League of America, 1983.

STONE, H. D., *Ready, Set, Go – An Agency Guide to Independent Living*, Washington, DC., Child Welfare League of America, 1987.

STONE, M. C., 'Foster Parents: Colleagues, Clients or Contractors?', *Child Care News*, June 1967.

SUSSER, E., STRUENING, E. L. and CONOVER, S. 'Childhood Experiences of Homeless Men', *American Journal of Psychiatry*, Dec. 1987, pp. 1599–1601.

SYLVA, K. and LUNT, I., *Child Development – A First Course*, London, Grant McIntyre, 1982.

TABER, M. A. and PROCH, K., 'Placement Stability for Adolescents in Foster Care: Findings from a Program Experiment', *Child Welfare*, vol. 66, no. 5, 1987, pp. 433–45.

TALBOT, N. (ED.) *Raising Children in Modern America*, Boston, Mass., Little, Brown, 1976.

THOBURN, J., MURDOCH, A. and O'BRIEN, A., *Permanence in Child Care*, Oxford and New York, Basil Blackwell, 1986.

THOMAS, M., 'Fostering Agreements: Taking Positive Steps', in Aldgate, J. (ed.) *Using Written Agreements With Children and Families*, London, Family Rights Group, 1988.

THORPE, R., 'The Experience of Children and Parents Living Apart', in Triseliotis, J. (ed.) *New Development in Adoption and Fostering*, London and Boston, Routledge and Kegan Paul, 1980, pp. 85–100.

TIMBERLAKE, E. M. and HAMLIN, E. R., 'The Sibling Group: A Neglected Dimension of Placement', *Child Welfare*, vol. 61, no. 8, 1982, pp. 545–60.

TIMBERLAKE, E. M. and VERDIECK, M. J., 'Psychosocial Functioning of Adolescents in Foster Care', *Social Casework*, vol. 68, no. 4, 1987, pp. 214–22.

TIZARD, B., *The Care of Young Children: Implications of Recent Research*, London, Thames Coram Research Unit, 1986.

TOWLE, C., 'Evaluating Motives of Foster Parents – Discussion', *Child Welfare*, vol. 31, no. 1, 1952; reprinted in Tod, R. J. N. (ed) *Social Work in Foster Care*, London, Longman, 1971.

TOZER, R., 'Treatment Fostering', *Adoption and Fostering*, vol. 3, no. 1, 1979, pp. 26–33.

TRASLER, G., *In Place of Parents*, London, Routledge and Kegan Paul, 1960.

TRISELIOTIS, J. 'Growing Up in Foster Care and After', in Triseliotis, J. (ed.)

New Developments in Foster Care and Adoption, London and Boston, Routledge and Kegan Paul, 1980, pp. 131–61.

TRISELIOTIS, J., 'Identity and Security', *Adoption and Fostering*, vol. 7, no. 1, 1983, p. 22–31.

TRISELIOTIS, J. (ed.) *Group Work in Adoption and Foster Care*, London, Batsford, 1988.

WHITE, M. S., 'Promoting Parent-Child Visiting in Foster Care: Continuing involvement within a Permanency Planning Framework', in Sinanoglu, P. A. and Maluccio, A. N. (eds) 1981, op. cit., pp. 461–75.

WHITTAKER, J. K. and GARBARINO, J., *Social Support Networks: Informal Helping in the Human Services*, New York, Aldine Publishing Company, 1983.

WHITTAKER, J. K., SCHINKE, S. P. and GILCHRIST, L. D., 'The Ecological Paradigm in Child, Youth, and Family Services: Implications for Policy and Practice', *Social Service Review*, vol. 60, no. 4, 1986, pp. 483–503.

WIEHE, V., 'The Foster Home Study: Evaluation or Preparation', paper presented at the National Association of Social Workers (NASW), Fifth Biennial Professional Symposium, San Diego, California, 1977.

WIMPFHEIMER, R. G., *Ageing out: A Child Welfare Dilemma of the 1980s*, unpublished dissertation, City University of New York, 1986.

WOODWARD, G., Letter to *Nottingham Foster Care Newsletter*, Spring 1986.

WOLINS, M., *Selecting Foster Parents: the Ideal and the Reality*, New York, Columbia University Press, 1963.

YELLOLY, M., *Social Work Theory and Psychoanalysis*, New York and London, Van Norstrand Reinhold, 1980.

ZIMMERMAN, R. B., *Foster Care in Retrospect*, Tulane Studies in Social Welfare, no. 14, New Orleans, Louisiana, 1982.

Name Index

Ahmed, S., 35, 36
Aldgate, J., 27, 30, 37, 45, 64, 65, 66, 67, 70, 71, 72, 73, 74, 89, 90, 91, 97, 120
Altorfer, J., 129
Ansell, D., 153, 156
Armor, D., 84
Association of British Adoption Agencies, 145
Aust, P., 70

Barnardo's New Families Project, 97, 100, 125
Barth, R. P., 90, 122, 123, 133, 137, 138
Bayless, K., 83, 136
Bayless, L., 156
Bennett, T., 94
Berkowitz, I. H., 100
Berridge, D., 42, 64, 65, 66, 68, 85, 89, 90, 94, 120
Berry, M., 90, 138
Bertsche, A. V., 88
Beyer, M., 123
Bland, D. C., 144
Blick, L. C., 100
Block, N. M., 120
Blumenthal, K., 88, 91
Boatman, B., 100
Borkan, E. L., 100
Borkman, R., 100
Bowlby, J. 37
Brady, J., 102, 104
Breakwell, G. M., 41
Brim, O., 35
Brin, M., 155
Brindis, C., 137
Brooks, J., 38

Bronfenbrenner, U., 36
Browne, A., 100
Brummer, N., 41
Bryant, B., 125, 152
Bullock, R., 22, 26, 71, 90
Burch, M., 74, 92, 93
Bush, M., 69

Cain, H., 71, 83, 85, 86
Carey, K., 15, 25, 26, 63, 64, 65, 66, 67, 69, 70, 71, 74, 75, 83, 85, 89, 122, 123, 135, 153
Cautley, P. W., 140
Cheetham, J., 35
Chestnut, M., 123
Child Welfare League of America, 34, 154
Clarke, G., 61, 62, 64
Clarke, F. W., 89
Clarkson, A., 124, 152
Clarren, J., 83, 136
Cleaver, H., 42, 64, 65, 66, 68, 85, 89, 90, 94, 120
Cole, E. P., 133
Collins, M. I., 14, 122
Collins, S. A., 102, 107
Colton, M., 67
Conover, S., 15
Cook, R., 153
Cordell, A. S., 97, 98
Corden, J. J., 102, 108
Cronbach, L. J., 58
Curtis Report, 141, 166

Davis, E., 158
Davis, I. P., 14, 100
Davis, L. J., 144

Subject Index